Whiteley's Bridge.

A SHORT HISTORY

OF THE

17th and 22nd Field Companies,

Third Sappers and Miners,

IN MESOPOTAMIA,

1914-1918.

The Naval & Military Press Ltd

Published by
The Naval & Military Press Ltd
5 Riverside, Brambleside, Bellbrook
Industrial Estate, Uckfield, East Sussex,
TN22 1QQ England

Tel: +44 (0) 1825 749494
Fax: +44 (0) 1825 765701

www.naval-military-press.com
www.military-genealogy.com

In reprinting in facsimile from the original, any imperfections are inevitably reproduced and the quality may fall short of modern type and cartographic standards.

BATTLE HONOURS.

Won by the

17th and 22nd Field Companies,

3rd Sappers and Miners,

1914-1916.

BASRA.
SHAIBA.
KUT-AL-AMARA 1915-1917.
CTESIPHON.
DEFENCE OF KUT-AL-AMARA.
MESOPOTAMIA.

CONTENTS.

Chapter.		Page.
I.	Mobilization up to the occupation of Basra.	1
II.	Engineer work in Basra.	9
III.	Advance to Qurna.	17
IV.	Shaiba.	22
V.	The Advance to Amara.	29
VI.	Halt at Amara.	34
VII.	Nasiriyeh.	38
VIII.	Kut-Al-Amara 1915. (Es-Sinn.) ...	42
IX.	Halt at Aziziyah and advance to Ctesiphon.	50
X.	Ctesiphon.	55
XI.	The Retreat to Kut-Al-Amara. ...	64
XII.	Siege of Kut-Al-Amara.—First Phase. Defence against the Turks.	71
XIII.	Defence of Kut-Al-Amara.—Second Phase. Defence against Flood.	89
XIV.	The Last Month.	104
XV.	Accounts by Subedar Mohammad Din, Bahadur, and Naik Govind Bikhaji Dhure of their captivity. ...	115

CONTENTS, *(Contd.)*

APPENDIX. PAGE.

I. Sappers and Miners Work at Basra. ... 15

II. Captain Matthews' account of the night march round the marshes. (Es-Sinn.) ... 48

III. Organization of Field Companies, Sappers and Miners in 1914. 125

IV. Statistics. 127

V. Honours and Distinctions Awarded. ... 130

LIST OF MAPS.

MAP NO.
1. Action at Sahil.
2. Basra—1914-15.
3. Qurna.
4. Shaiba.
5. Operations near Nasiriya, July 1915.
6. Kut-Al-Amara 27th and 28th September 1915.
7. Battle of Ctesiphon 22nd November 1915.
8. The Defence of Kut-Al-Amara.
9. Kut-Al-Amara. —Flood Defences.
10. Lower Mesopotamia.

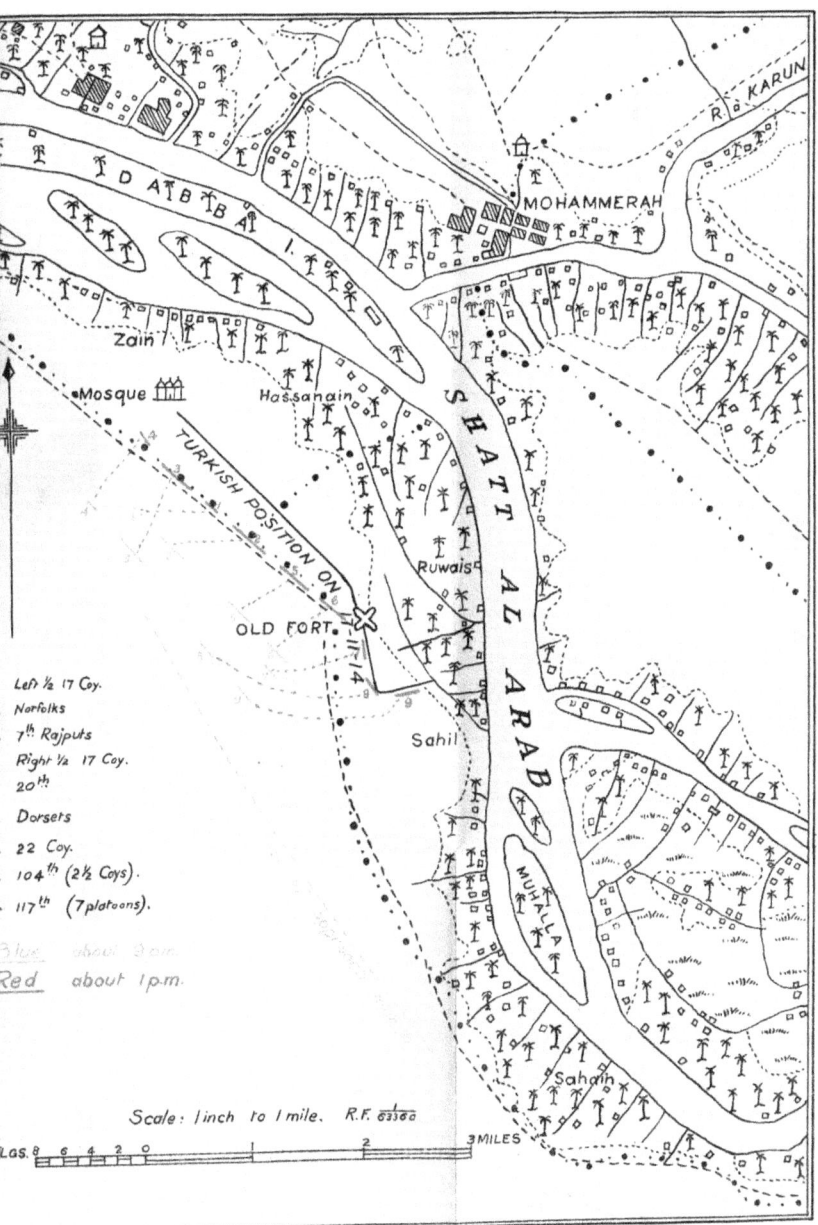

Map I — Action at SAHIL

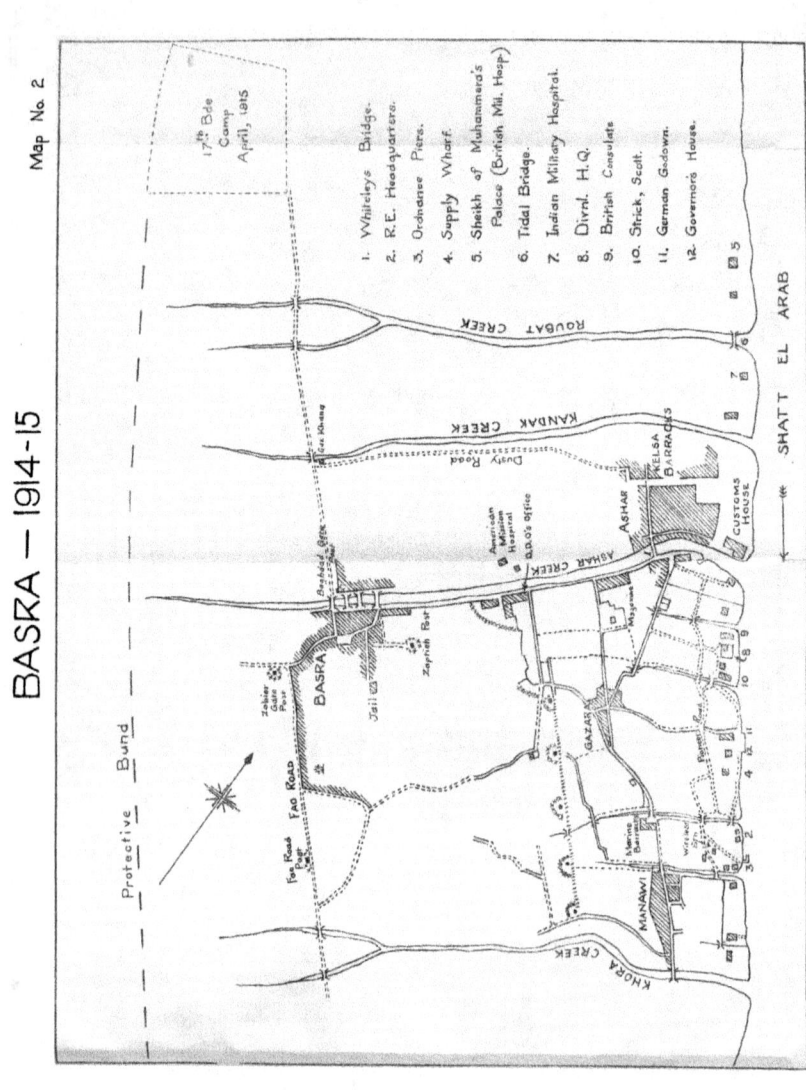

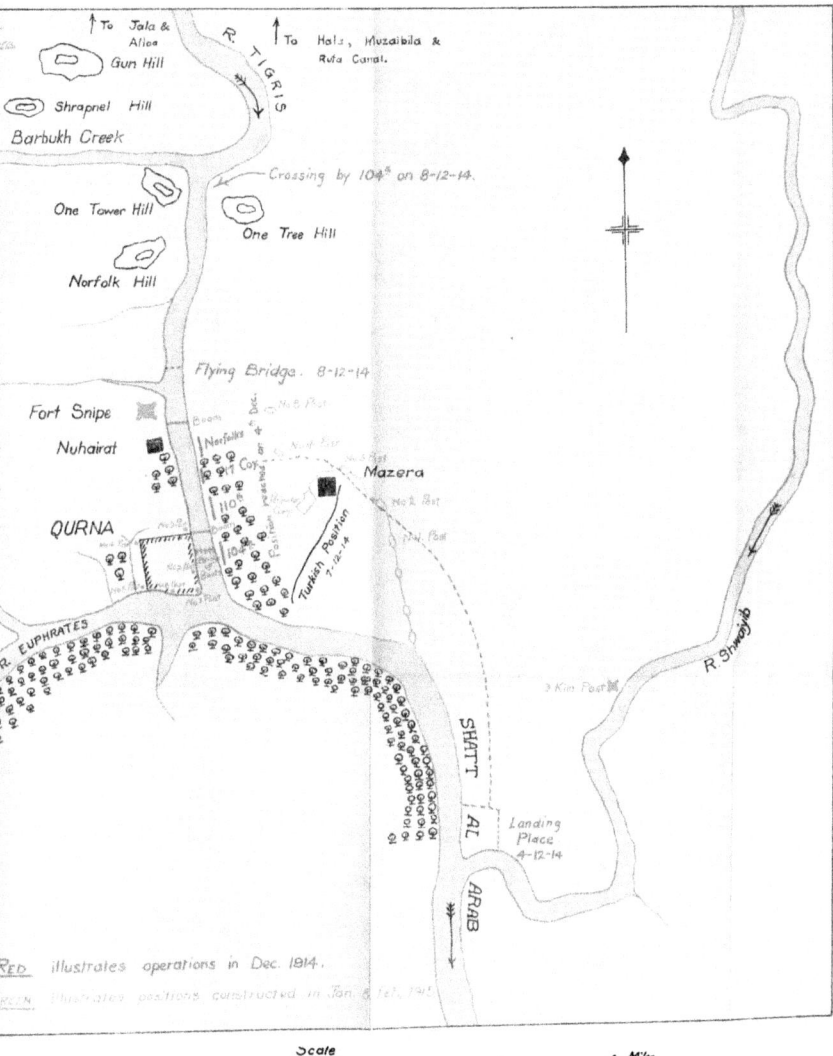

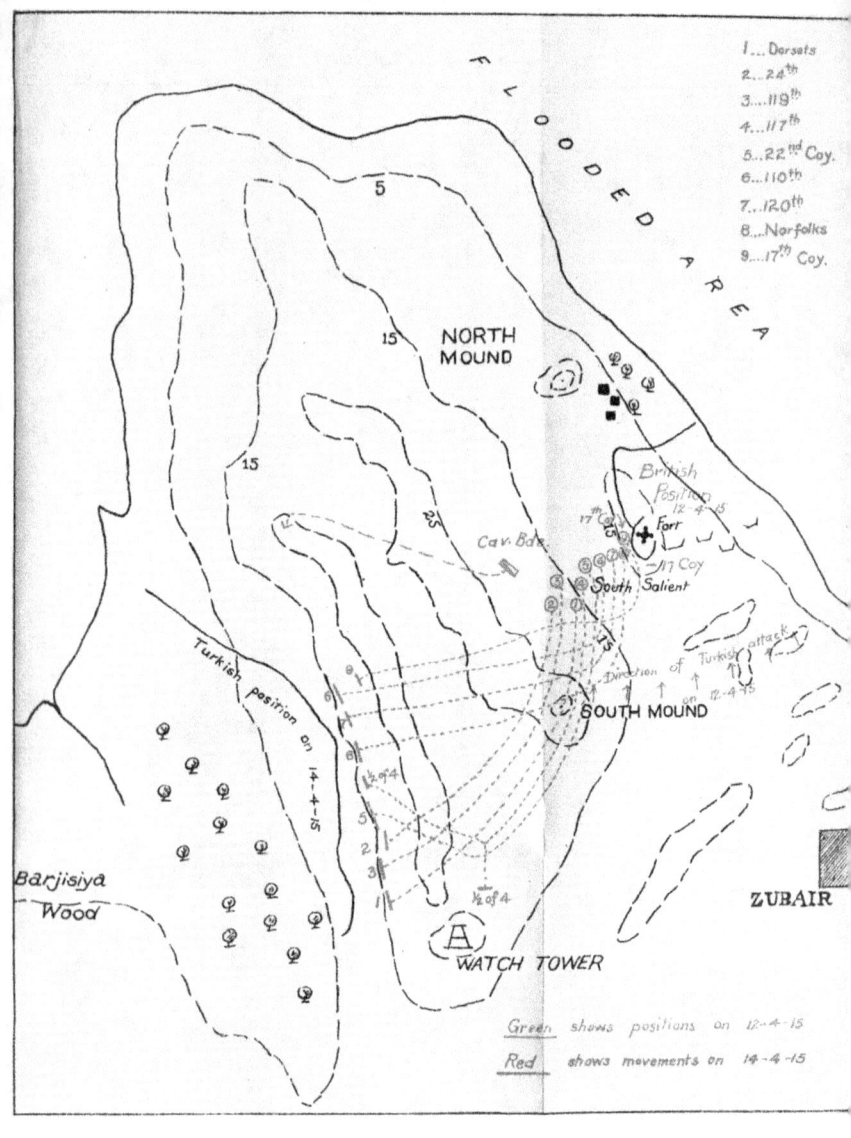

OPERATIONS NEAR NASIRIYA
JULY 1915

Map 5

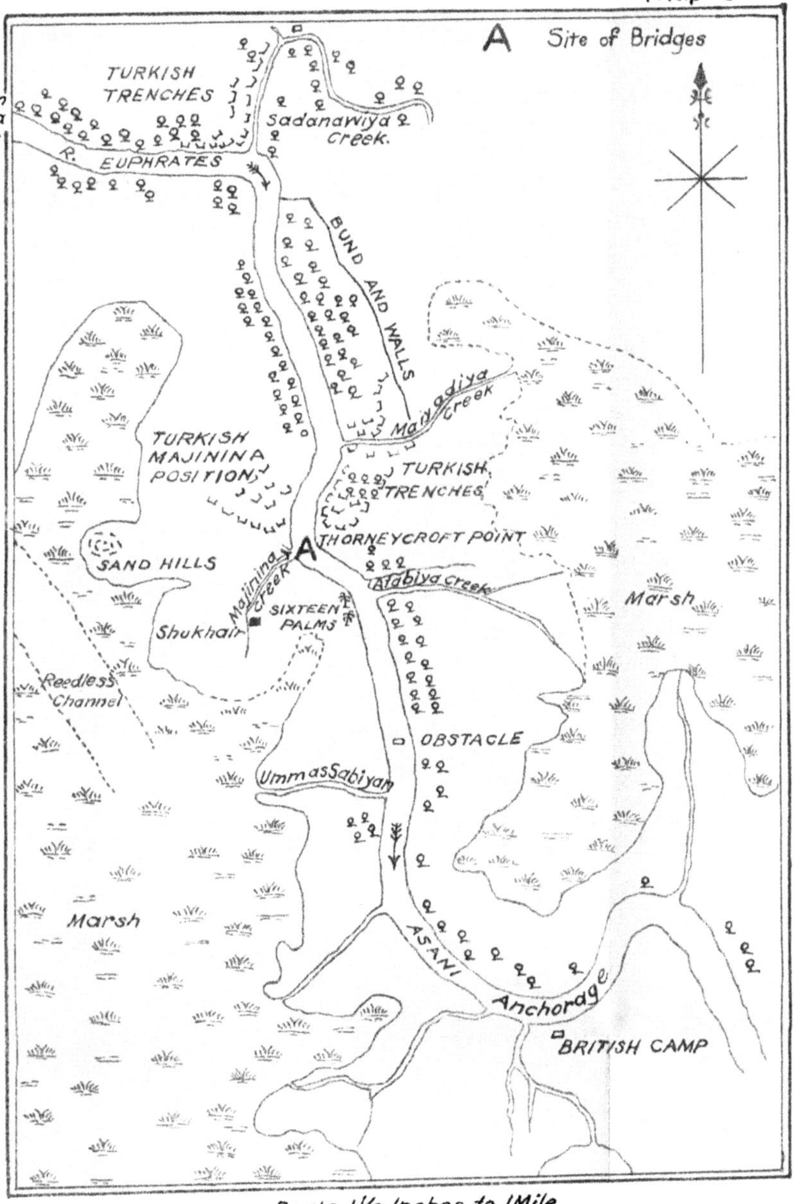

Scale 1½ Inches to 1 Mile

MILE 1 ¾ ½ ¼ 0 1 2 MILES

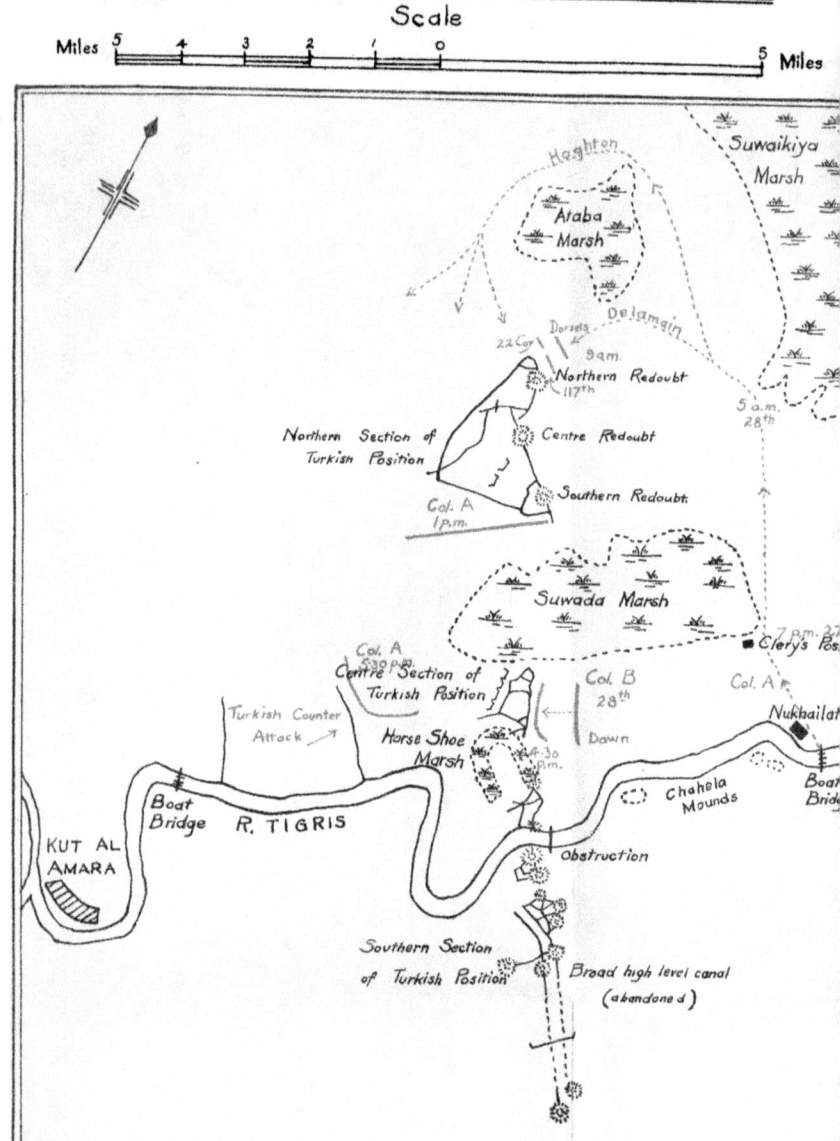

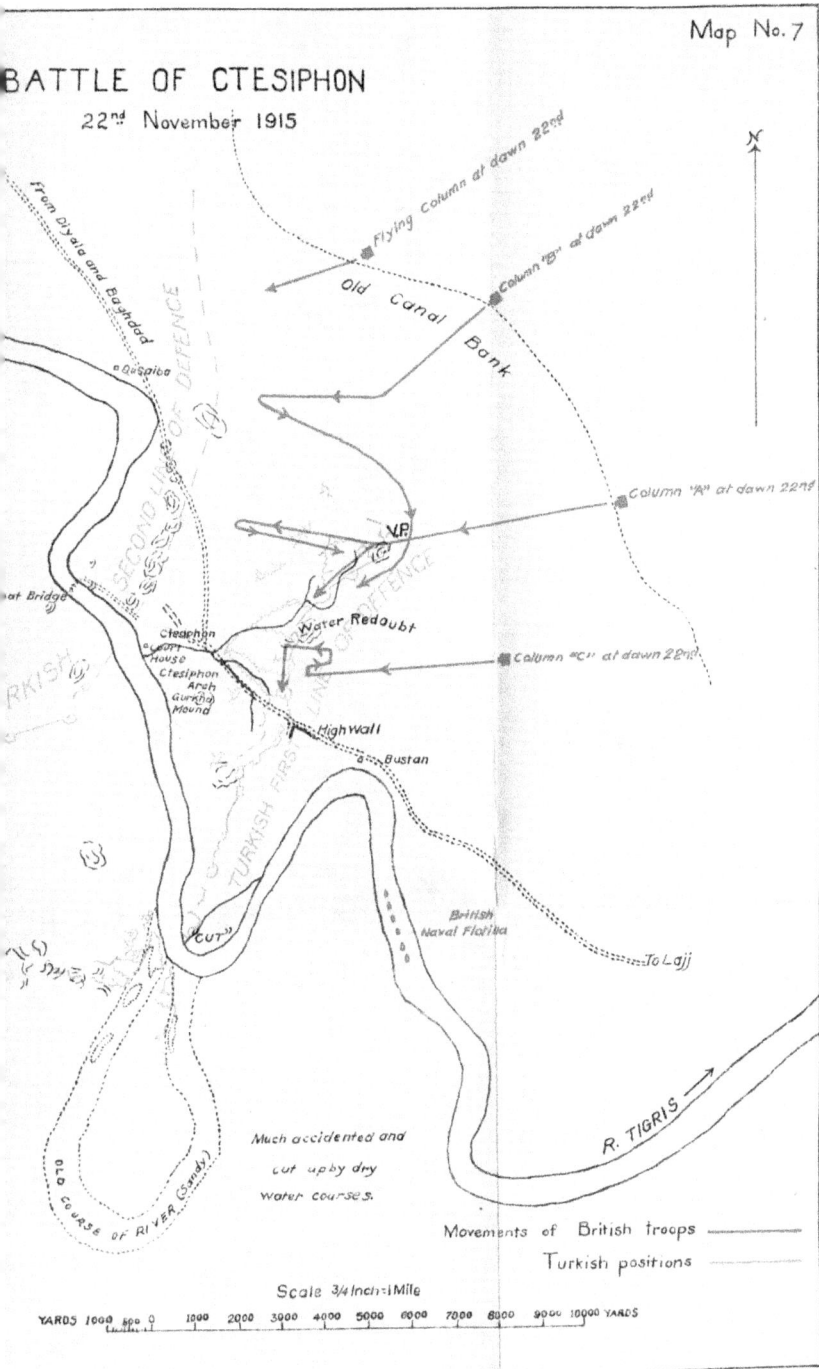

The Defence of Kut Al Amara

Map

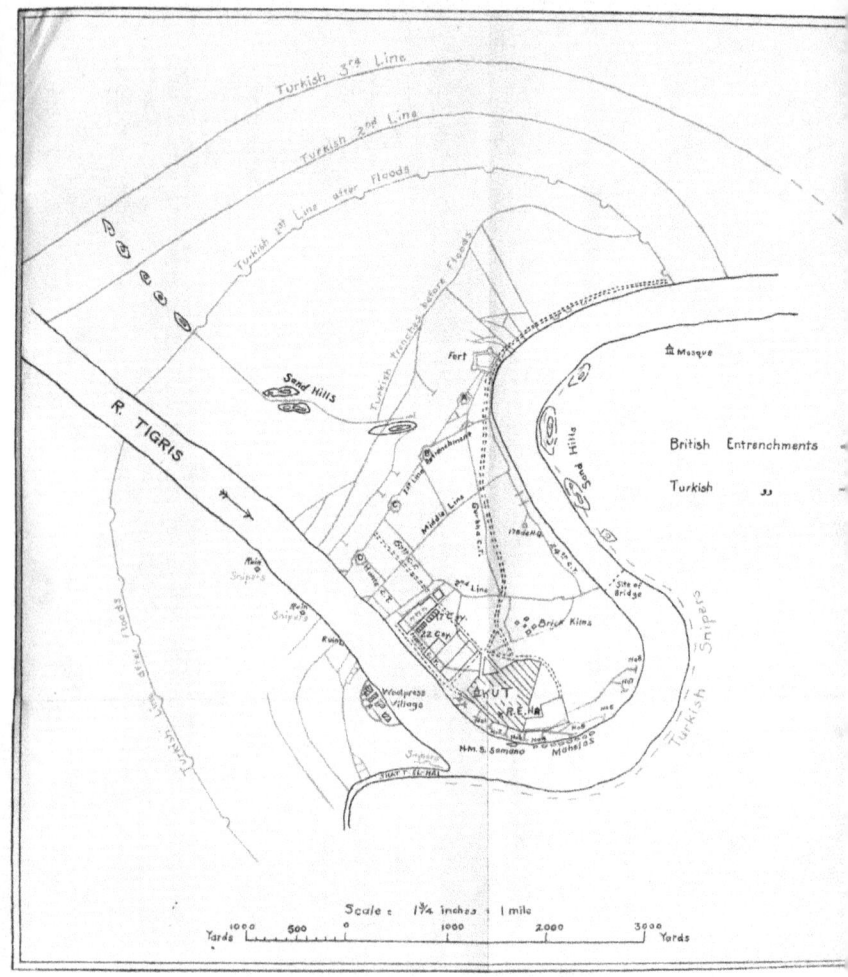

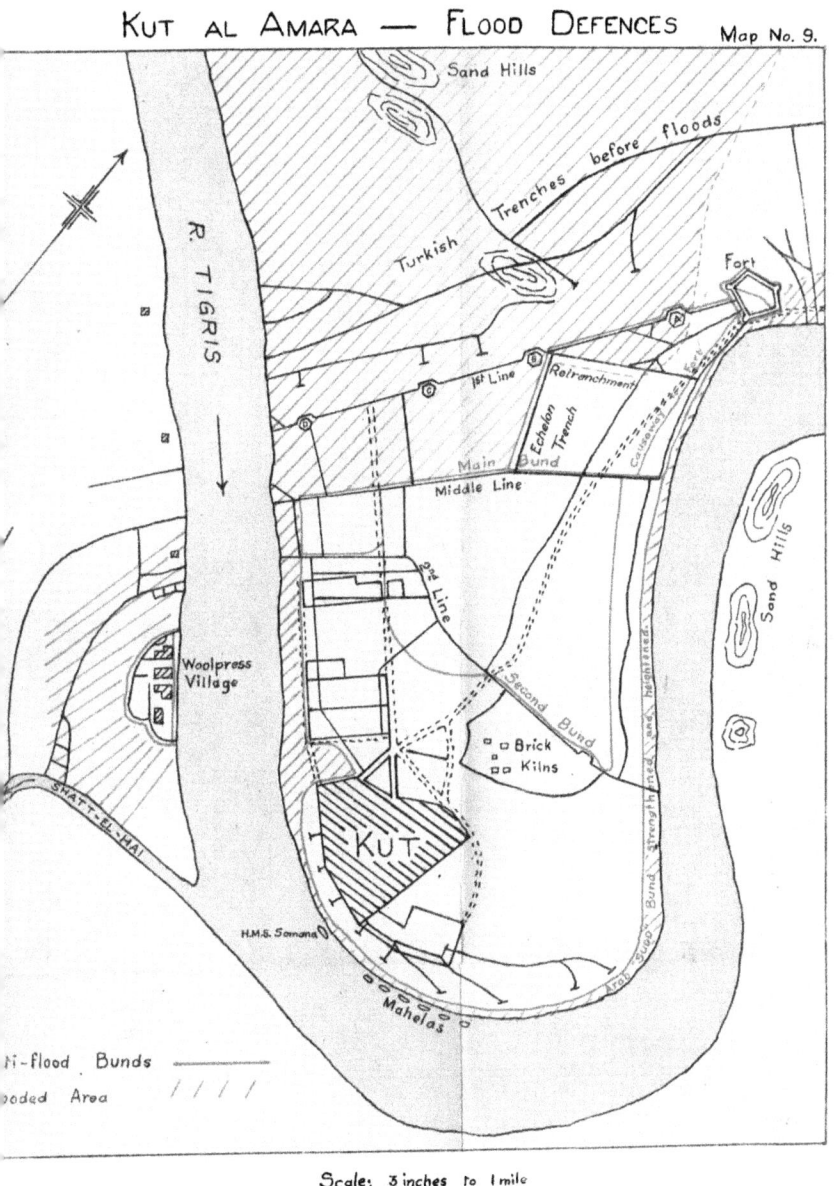

LOWER MESOPOTAMIA

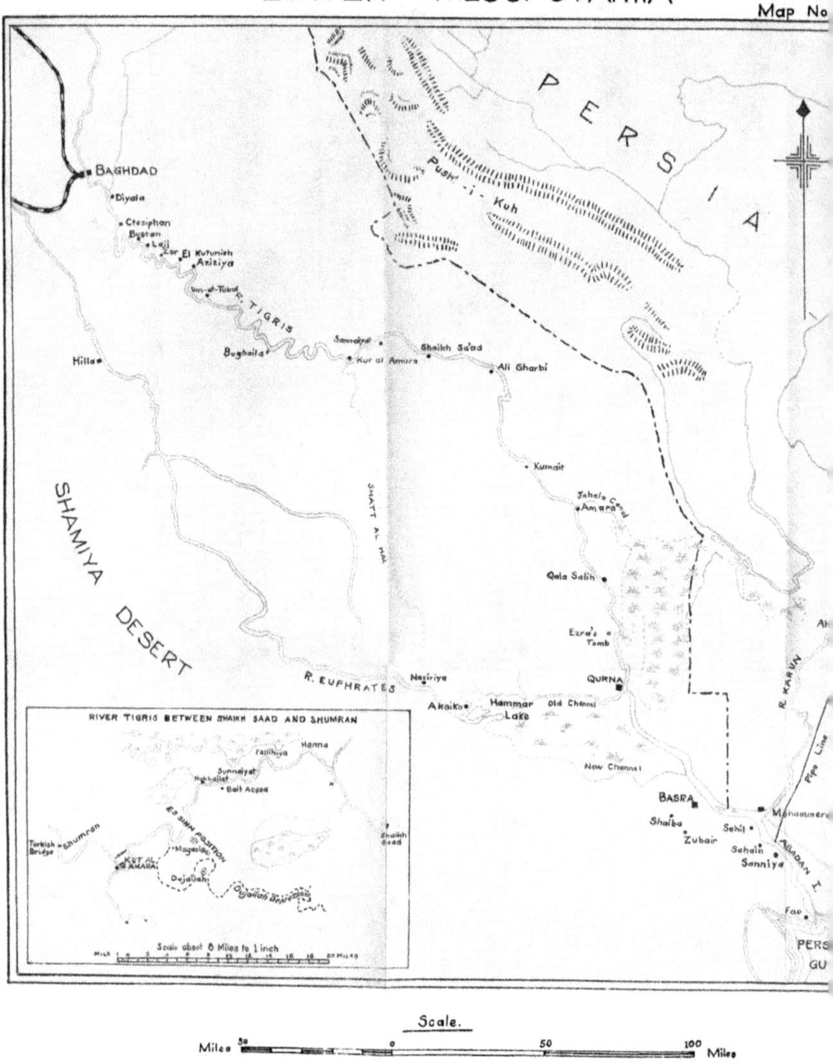

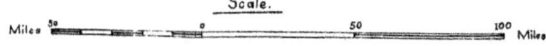

CORRIGENDA.

Introduction, first page, lines 6 and 35 *for* Sandys *read* Sandes.

Page   6 line 18 *for* Whitely *read* Whiteley.
Page   6 line 19 *for* Arbuthnott *read* Arbuthnot.
Page   7 line 8 *for* Jamdare *read* Jamdade.
Page 18 line 33 *for* Gulam *read* Ghulam.
           line 34 *for* Haider *read* Haidar
Page 28 line 29 *for* Arbuthnctt *read* Arbuthnot.
Page 41 line 24 *for* Ali Ghabi *read* Ali Gharbi.
Page 43 line 35 *for* were *read* went.
Page 58 line 41 *for* right *read* left.
Page 59 line 24 *for* on *read* nearer.
Page 83 line 39 *for* Basra *read* Amara.
Page 95 last line *for* norations *read* no rations.
Page 106 line 7 *for* meal *read* day.
Page 112 line 4 *for* particularly *read* practically.
Page 115 line 23 *for* Shumran *read* Samarra.
Page 131 line 22 *for* combined *read* considered.

INTRODUCTION.

It is eighteen years since the 6th (Poona) Division embarked for Mesopotamia, and sixteen since it was forced by starvation to surrender at Kut-Al-Amara. The story of its achievements can be read in the Official History of the war and Gen. Townshend's "My Campaign in Mesopotomia," while other books, the best of which is perhaps Col. Sandys' "In Kut and Captivity," give of the story of the campaign from a more personal point of view. An attempt has here been made to write a short history of the two companies of the 3rd Sappers & Miners, who formed part of the engineers of the 6th Division. The work of these divisional engineers is perhaps unique. Under the direction of the divisional engineer commander, they had to perform, generally with improvised materials, almost every kind of work which at that time could be expected from engineer troops : and also owing to the weakness of the force, they frequently found themselves acting as infantry in attack and defence. Their record seems worth preserving. The officers of the 3rd Sappers and Miners who survived the war are now rapidly disappearing from the active list. The opportunity is therefore taken, before it is too late, of collating their reminescences into narrative form.

The engineer troops of the 6th Division were the 17th and 22nd Field Companies, 3rd Sappers and Miners, and the 48th Pioneers. The division was luckier than most Indian divisions in that all its engineer troops were stationed together at Kirkee, where also was the engineer commander designate, the commandant of the 3rd Sappers and Miners. Consequently these troops had excellent opportunities of training together and were all well known to the divisional commander and his staff at Poona, four miles away. To them were added later the Sirmur Imperial Service Sappers and Miners and the Bridging Train of the 1st (King George's Own) Sappers and Miners. It would, no doubt, be of great technicial interest to write a history of these divisional engineers as a whole. The story of the Bridging Train has been admirably told by Colonel Sandys, but otherwise the records available only permit the compiler to deal with the two 3rd Sappers and Miners companies.

These records are the war diaries (incomplete) of the two companies, the narratives of work maintained in the divisional engineer commander's office up to May, 1915, and the personal recollections of Brigadier General U. W. Evans, C.B., C.M.G., Colonel F. A. Wilson, C.B., Lieut.-Colonel E. J. Loring, M.C., Major K. B. S. Crawford, Major K. D. Yearsley, M.C., Captain A. B. Matthews, D.S.O., M.C., Major L. W. H. Mathias, D.S.O., (I.A.S.C.). and Mr. W. R. Boyes, late I.A.R.O. Enough has been extracted from the Official History to make the story of the companies intellegible. It is believed that there is nothing in this book which is not based on the above records.

When the great war broke out, the Third Sappers and Miners were a particularly happy family. The Officers and British and Indian other ranks pulled well together and the esprit de corps was very strong. The four field companies stationed at Kirkee and an improvised bridging train were mobilized in the first few weeks of the war; the 20th and 21st Field Companies went to France in August with the 3rd (Lahore) Division, the 17th and 22nd Field Companies to Mesopotamia with the 6th (Poona) Division, and the Bridging Train to East Africa. Later the remaining existing companies of the Corps and many newly raised units took part in the war, but the first four field companies bore the brunt, and it is a proud fact that, apart from individual distinctions, all four were mentioned for gallantry in the body of a dispatch by the Commanders-in-Chief of the forces with which they were employed. The 17th and 22nd Field Companies had the misfortune to become, with the rest of the Poona Division, prisoners of war in April, 1916, but they certainly had a brilliant share in winning their Royal title for their Corps, which is now known as the Royal Bombay Sappers and Miners.

CHAPTER I.

Mobilization up to the occupation of Basra.

The 22nd Field Company was mobilized on 9th September, 1914. The officers and British N.C.Os. of the company were :—

    Capt. A. M. Twiss, R.E.
    Lieut. C. M. G. Dunhill, R.E.
    ,, E. C. Whiteley, R.E.
    ,, A. B. Matthews, R.E.
    Sub. . Keru Jamdade.
    Jem. Firoz Ali.
    ,, Ramswami Naidu.
    Sergt. Bellis, R.E.
    ,, Arter, R.E.

The Company embarked on H.T. Varela at Bombay on 16th October, 1914, forming part of the advanced detachment of the 6th (Poona) Division under the command of Brigadier General W. S. Delamain and consisting of the 16th Infantry Brigade (2nd Dorsets, 104th Rifles, 117th Mahrattas and 20th Punjabis), 1st Indian Mountain Artillery Brigade and 22nd Company. The Division had originally been mobilized for service in France, but though, on departure, the destination was unknown, it soon became evident that it was the Persian Gulf. The transports actually arrived at Bahrein on 23rd October, where they remained till the 2nd of November. The weather was very hot and the troops being kept on board had an uncomfortable time. The Sappers, however, were kept busy with preparations for the eventual disembarkation; eight life boats were fitted with floor boards to take mules; H.T. Varela was fortified, the bulwarks of two decks being rendered bullet proof with breastworks of twelve inches of coal between corrugated sheet iron and furnished with traverses and emplacements for mountain and machine guns. The horses and mules on board were protected with similar barricades of bales of compressed hay; and gang planks and kerosine oil tin rafts were also constructed.

Assistance was also given in fortifying H.T. Umaria. The remarks of the captain when informed by Matthews, that he had been sent to put coal between corrugated iron on his bridge, cannot unfortunately be recorded. Neither the captain nor his chief officer, who came up to his aid, seemed to mind if all the soldiery in general, and the Sappers in particular, got shot, but they did want their bridge clean.

On 3rd November, the convoy picked up pilots at Bushire and on the 4th arrived outside the bar of the Shat-Al-Arab. On the 6th, after the naval escort had silenced the Turkish shore guns at Fao, the two fortified transports passed up stream and landed the 117th Mahrattas and a section of sappers under Dunhill and Matthews. There was no opposition and the troops re-embarked, Dunhill remaining with a few sappers and some infantry to destroy the fort and throw into the river the four guns which had engaged the ships.

On the 7th, the transports proceeded up river to Abadan, and on the 8th, 9th and 10th the force disembarked at Sanniya, about 20 miles above the bar, on the right (Turkish) bank of the river and some 30 miles below Basra. The 22nd Company was employed for some days making roads and small bridges over irrigation channels in the camp area and ramps for unloading guns, which were constructed from the ships' hatch covers.

Meanwhile, the 17th Field Company, which had been mobilized at the same time, left Kirkee on 5-11-14 and embarked on H. T. Aronda, at Bombay, on 6-11-14. (The mules embarked separately on H. T. Erinpura.)

The Officers and B.N.C.Os. with the company were :—

Capt. A. D. S. Arbuthnot, R.E.,
Lieut. R. C. Lord, R.E.,
„ M. G. Gunning Campbell, R.E.,
„ K. B. S. Crawford, R.E.,
Subr. Baryam Singh, I.O.M.,
Jem. Ganpatrao Jadhao.
„ Muhammad Din.
Sergt. Toleman, R.E.,
„ Baker, R.E.,

Lt-Col. U. W. Evans, R.E., Commandant, Third Sappers and Miners, who had been appointed Divisional Engineer Commander, accompanied this part of the force. With him were Capt. H. W. Tomlinson, R.E., his adjutant, and Major A. R. Winsloe, R.E., and Capt. F. C. Molesworth, R.E., field engineers.

They sailed on 7th November and anchored off the bar of the Shat-Al-Arab at 6-30 a.m. on 13th. Next day the transports went up stream to Sanniya, and at 4 p.m. the right half company disembarked with Arbuthnot and Crawford and bivouacked, the other half company and the mules landing on the 15th. During the remainder of the day and the 16th they assisted the disembarkation of the other troops (33rd Cavalry, 10th Brigade R.F.A., 18th Indian Infantry Brigade and 48th Pioneers).

Here Arbuthnot displayed great ingenuity on landing animals. Many horses and mules had been lowered into deep undecked boats and when these reached the bank there was no means of getting them out. Arbuthnot built a ramp of hay bales against the inside of the boat and after many struggles the animals climbed the almost perpendicular twelve or fifteen feet.

On the 15th, part of the 16th Brigade attacked a Turkish force of about the same strength in position at Sahain, five miles up the river, and forced them to evacuate their position which they did not re-occupy. 22nd Company was not engaged. On the 16th, Lt. Gen. Sir A. Barrett, the Divisional Commander who was now in command, decided to move the camp up stream, so as to be in a better position to safeguard the Shaikh of Mohammerah, our ally on the opposite bank. The whole force consequently moved out from Sanniya towards the north west at 5-15 a.m. on the 17th, marching clear of the thick belt of date palms fringing the river.

For this operation, the Divisional Engineer Commander allotted the 17th Company to the 18th Brigade and the 22nd Company to the 16th Brigade. Whiteley, with one section of the latter company, was detailed to take up stream a mahela (i.e., a large local lighter), loaded with material for landing facilities. The D.E.C's. instructions were that whenever sapper companies were allotted to brigades during an offensive action a sapper officer and a section should always be well up so that the ground might be studied and places chosen for rallying points, and other defensive measures taken in co-operation with the brigade staffs, before the main body of the company, held back in rear, arrived. Generally, however, by the time the assault was delivered, the Sappers were in the front line.

The 17th Company marched at the head of the main guard, the Sappers carrying cutting tools, and the 22nd

Company near the head of the main body. After passing the old Turkish position at Sahain, our cavalry found the enemy holding trenches on the edge of the groves, their line (about 2 miles long) being parallel to the river, and our line of march and their left apparently marked by an old fort. The march continued till the advanced guard was roughly opposite the enemy's right, when both brigades (16th on right and 18th on left) faced to their right and swung in to attack covered by the artillery. The ground in front of the position was dead flat and entirely devoid of cover, and an intense rainstorm fell during the march and continued at intervals during the action. As a result the mud was appalling; it was almost impossible to drag one's feet out of it and the field artillery could only move at a walk.

On the right, the 16th Brigade attacked, with the Dorsets directed at the fort and the 20th Punjabis on their left. The 22nd Company followed the Dorsets, the sappers carrying demolition charges with which it was proposed to destroy the fort. It was, however, soon found that the enemy's line extended a mile or more south of the fort, and the 104th Rifles and part of the 117th Marathas, who were in support, were sent to the right to find and turn this flank. The 22nd Company came up on the Dorsets right to fill the gap and so found itself attacking in the first line in the middle of the brigade. The attack developed exactly on the lines of pre-war manœuvres. The enemy on this flank were Turkish regulars who began to fire at about 1000 yards range. Progress was slow at first. Twiss was mortally wounded and the Subedar also hit, and the company was led on by Matthews and Jemadar Firoz Ali. As the flank attack made itself felt, the Dorsets and 22nd Company closed in, and at 1.15 p.m. charged on to the position, the Turks bolting. Some sappers with Matthews and Jemadar Firoz Ali were the first troops to reach the trench, Naik Dalip Singh being the first arrival and himself shooting three Turks as they were leaving. The 16th Brigade were now at right angles to their original line of advance and swept up the belt of date groves, but the heavy going prevented rapid movement.

The 22nd Company was, by this time, pretty well mixed up with the Dorsets, and went on with them in a northerly direction, firing when targets presented themselves till it was evident that the survivors of the enemy had got clear. Matthews then remembered the demolition charges, collected his men and went back to destroy the fort; but it was found to be only a heap of dried mud, not worth a few slabs of guncotton.

Meanwhile, on the left, the 18th Brigade prolonged the attack. The Norfolks were leading with the 7th Rajputs in support. At first the 17th Company was used as escort to the mountain guns (a role very reminiscent of pre-war field days) but before the attack developed, it was moved up into line with the infantry, the left half with Arbuthnot and Lord on the left of the Norfolks, and the right half under Campbell on the left of the Rajputs. (Crawford was acting as galloper to the 18th Brigade Commander). The enemy (here Arab levies) opened fire at about 1500 yards and the Rajputs, with Campbell's half company, came up on the Norfolks left. The advance continued for about 800 yards during which Arbuthnot and four sappers were wounded. At this point the 16th Brigade's attack had driven the Turks out of their position on the left, and the Arabs in front of the 18th Brigade quitted *en masse*, affording an excellent rapid fire target for the company.

This first experience of the Arabs instilled our men with great contempt for them. Later they learned also to hate them for their double faced behaviour—sentiments which were largly shared by the Turks.

By 3 p.m. the whole of the Turkish position had been occupied and the force was withdrawn into bivouac at Sahil. The D.E.C., Lieut. Col. Evans, had been hit in the leg (which necessitated his spending the next fortnight on the hospital ship) and the command of the divisional engineers devolved on Major Winsloe, who put the Sappers on to work as soon as they reached the bivouac site about 5 p.m. The 17th Company were employed on a road through the bivouac, the chief work being filling in irrigation channels. This was finished about 7.30 p.m.

The 22nd Company was detailed to make a pier to evacuate the wounded to the ships. The tide was low and the foreshore was a vast expanse of mud; beyond which the ships could be dimly seen far away on the gale swept river. The Sappers started to fell date palms to make a causeway and went on till very late, but no wounded were embarked till next day.

On first bringing his men to the pier site, Matthews found crowds of wounded awaiting attention by the overworked medical officers. There was a group of sappers on the outskirts with a stretcher on which lay Twiss, who had been shot through the stomach. Matthews went to the medical officer and asked if he had room for Twiss in his one and only small tent. The reply was: "I shall have it in a minute. There is a man here who is bound to die soon. He hasn't an earthly hope". The man in question was Arbuthnot! The medical officer told Matthews that Twiss had a very good chance of living.

It was a bitterly cold night and every one's teeth were chattering.

Twiss died of his wounds next day. He was buried by his brother officers and Indian officers. Whiteley and his section had just got ashore on the edge of the open desert a few yards from the palm groves. Twiss had served 12 years with the Third Sappers and Miners, four of them as adjutant and had commanded the 22nd Company for four years. He was universally liked and was a great loss. In Dunhill's absence, Whitely took command.

Arbuthnott, however, was not yet to die. He had been hit by a large bore bullet which traversed his body and lodged near his pelvis. He was taken on board the Varela, now a hospital ship, and a week later was able to tell off Matthews, when he visited him, for holding morbid conversations with the medical officer over his stretcher at Sahil. He was invalided to India and thence to England. He joined the 20th Field Company, 3rd Sappers and Miners, in France, brought it out to Mesopotamia at the end of 1915, and was killed under circumstances of great gallantry in the Dujailah redoubt in March 1916. By his death the Corps lost a very capable and gallant officer. A man of fine physique, he was fond of all sports and games; he was a good polo player, boxer and oar, and a successful shikari.

He was of a keen and forceful character, never happy unless he was trying something new, the more dangerous the better.

On one occasion he expressed a desire to the commandant to swim his company, clothed and carrying their arms, across the river at Kirkee. The commandant told him to take a sapper or two and a boat and himself swim the river so equipped before he could give permission. Shortly after he come back and said it was child's play. Permission was given but it must be recorded that the company spent some time fishing various rifles from the bottom of the river.

Subadar Keru Jamdade was also invalided to India. The other casualties were:—

17th Company, 4 I.O.R. wounded.
22nd   ,,   4 ,,   killed and 16 wounded.

In connection with the action, Lieut. A. B. Matthews was awarded the Military Cross and Jemadar Firoz Ali and Naik Dalip Singh the Indian Order of Merit, 2nd class.

As a result of the invaliding of Subadar Keru Jamdare, Jemadar Firoz Ali was promoted Subedar and Havaldar Tek Singh Jemadar.

From the 18th to the 21st the force remained in camp at Sahil. The companies were employed on roads in camp and landing arrangements. Small jetties were made with crib piers, constructed with palm logs and a track of palm fronds laid across the mud at low tide ending in a ramp of fodder bales to land guns and animals. The ramp vanished when the tide rose. On the 20th, No. 1 Section, 17th Company, moved by water to Sanniya, where they used all the available sand bags in building a ramp to disembark horses. It was then decided to land the horses at Sahil after all, and as all available material had been disposed of, they were jumped from the lighters on to palm leave tracks. Guns could only be landed at high tide.

During this period also, the 22nd Company put the old fort at Sahil into a state of defence. No water supply work was done by the companies, but they lent all their lift and force pumps to the troops.

News that the Turks had evacuted Basra was received on the 20th, and on the 21st our gunboats steamed up and put a stop to the looting going on by Arabs. Part of the 18th Brigade followed them by river early on the 22nd. The main body marched from Sahil at 8 p.m. on 21st, 17th Company near the head of the main body. During this march (32 miles), both companies were busy making roadways across the numerous irrigation channels. The force arrived on the south west outskirts of the city at noon on the 22nd, and the companies bivouacked at 2 p.m. They immediately got their pumps into action and started improving communications in the camp. The night march had been trying, but as soon as the sun rose, everyone was in the best of spirits.

On the 23rd a ceremonial entry was made into Basra, one section of 17th Company and the whole of 22nd Company taking part, and in the afternoon the two companies moved into billets at the German Consulate at Ashar, the river quarter of Basra. On the 26th, they again moved to the Turkish Commodore's House, which gave improved accommodation. This building remained R. E. Headquarters at Basra throughout the war and the inscribed stone originally over the gateway is now in the Royal Bombay Sappers and Miners' Mess at Kirkee.

CHAPTER II.

Engineer work in Basra.

From the day of arrival, engineer work proceeded continuously in Basra. The base had to be put into a state of defence, communications improved and landing facilities of all kinds provided. The work allotted to the field companies by the D.E.C. was assisting the infantry in defence works (principally wiring and overhead cover), bridging across the numerous creeks and work on piers and jetties.

The companies were on this work as follows:—

17th Company 22-11-14—2-12-14. (half company till
15-12-1914).
29-4-15—16-7-15.
10-8-15—16-8-15.
22nd Company 22-11-14—6-4-15.
21-4-15—27-5-15.

These periods include a certain number of days in May spent in preparing material for the advance from Qurna.

Appendix 1 contains a list of some of the work done by the companies during these periods. Local resources in materials were very limited, but there was a large store of timber belonging to a German firm and consisting of many thousands of square feet of deal scantlings and planks. Capt. F. C. Molesworth, R.E. organized an engineer field park quickly and efficently. Nevertheless, engineer work at Basra during this period was always a case of making such material as was available do. The trestles and superstructure of piers, and bridges were almost invariably composed of two inch planking. Such structures, especially the piers, were easily damaged and repairs were constantly required, though later light piles were available and were driven round the piers to carry a protective framework. But the work done was of the utmost value. It formed the basis for the unloading and transportation work of the base until well on in 1916, when with more labour and materials, 12 inch piles and heavy R.S.Js. began to replace the planking of 1915, and a port authority, headed by an eminent harbour engineer, began to build wharves for ocean going steamers. Until then and including the period of expansion in early 1916, the work of the base and the maintenance of the force largely depended on the work done by the companies in early 1915. Most of their structures were in use till the end of the war and many are to the present date. The bulk of the work was done by 22nd Company, as 17th Company moved to Qurna early in December.

Demands for landing stages were found to follow an inevitable routine. Each started with: "will you please construct a light floating stage to disembark a few men, or for the use of staff motor boats or bellums?" This having been done, a few days later there came: "will you please make your last stage safe for landing a few stores?" The next step was: "will you please fix it for a few horses?" Lastly "will you please put a head on it so that we can pile up stores ready to load on to boats?" In the end, the O.C. 22nd Company decided that when his company was ordered to build anything, whether pier or bridge, it should be calculated to take a load of "galloping elephants, crowded at a check" (the original specification has been bowlderized to suit the printed word).

Some of the works required considerable ingenuity. The footbridge constructed by the 22nd Company across the Robat Creek, which divided the British from the Indian Hospital, was a case in point. The creek was 100 feet wide, the tide ran at four knots and had a rise and fall of four feet. A constant stream of barges—always with the tide—had to be passed through, but as no personnel could be spared to work a cut, the latter had to be automatic.

The outer ends of the shore bays, were supported on barrel rafts, which were held in position by distance pieces hinged to holdfasts at half tide level. To these rafts the main members of the bridge (two forty-foot loading ramps) were hinged on vertical pivots. Each of the midstream ends was supported on a raft from which a rope ran round a pulley, fastened to the bottom of the canal, and was held taut by a counter weight ashore. When a barge came along it pushed the two halves apart and when it had passed, the counter weights pulled them together again.

The I.M.S. officers returning to their hospital after dinner had some thrilling adventures and several cold baths, as there was no hand rail. Even by day, crossing the centre point was apt to be a little speculative as the gap varied and the surface was sometimes slippery. The strong current added interest to the passage. The bridge, however, was in constant use and never suffered any damage from the barges which had nothing to do but crash through.

The erection of gallows is not taught as military engineering, but became a fairly common work in Mesopotamia. Two single gallows were at first erected in Basra but failed to meet the demand, so a gallows to hang four criminals simultaneously was erected. Matthews records that "while building this gallows, we were working before a denser and more critical crowd than I ever played before at Twickenham. The annoyance, when he boxed in the place for the men to drop into, could be felt. I thought at one time, the crowd would try and take the boxing off." "This gallows was brought into use the moment it was finished, but after its efficiency had been proved, the demand fell off and for the first time in three hundred years, Basra was not raided at full moon." It was also recorded that a certain imbecile who spent most of his time in the Sooq (quarter) where the gallows were, and who, as always in the East, was looked upon with pity and consideration as being nearer to Heaven than other men, took up his lodging in the covered drop, and was found dead there one morning.

Flood control is an unusual R.E. service. The Shat-Al-Arab rises in February and March and reaches its peak at the beginning of April. "Bunds" are made up annually along the banks of the main river and also of the creeks and many of the smaller distributaries. The Arabs are experts at making up these bunds, using a special kind of impermeable mud, known by a weed which grows in it. Not only has the Shat-Al-Arab to be kept at bay, but the Euphrates overflows into the desert west of Basra (as was very much in evidence at the time of the Shaiba battles) and had to be guarded against.

The D.E.C. took Crawford out of his company and put him in charge of flood control with plenty of Arab labour and rupees. Previous flood levels were ascertained and all bunds guarding the base area built up to a foot above previous record height. But when the flood came, it beat all previous records; the foot clearence became two or three inches and gave Crawford many anxious moments; but at only one spot were his defences pierced and that was immediately reported by his watchers and remedied in a few hours.

The 17th Brigade, however, in camp near the end of the Robat Creek, on the north bank, had undertaken their own defence against the desert flood. One night a westerly storm piled up this flood against and over their bund, and after a losing battle of three hours against the water, the whole brigade was forced to evacuate their position and retire across the creek.

The finest job done by the divisional engineers in Basra was undoubtedly the bridge built by part of the 22nd Company in February, 1915, over the Ashar Creek on the site of an old Turkish bridge. Naval divers first blew out the footings of the old bridge and caused a great sensation among the local inhabitants. The new bridge was 110 feet long and designed to take $5\frac{1}{2}$ ton axle loads and consisted of two short shore spans, four spans of 19 feet, and a central span of 27 feet. The roadway was carried on two pairs of continuous girders, each cantilevered 9 feet over the central span. The central nine feet was a counter-weighted lifting span. The girders were 53 inches deep, each flange consisting of four 8 inch by 3 inch planks, bolted and strapped together, and the web two layers of 1 inch boarding laid at 45^0 slope nailed on to each side. The trestles were made of 10 inch by $1\frac{1}{2}$ inch planks, four being bolted together for each leg. Fourteen roadbearers 8 inch by 3 inch were used on each bay, supported by 12 inch by 6 inch cross beams (either solid or made up of planks) resting on the lower boom. Transverse bracing was afforded to the superstruture by angle iron frame bolted to the transoms and to the outside of the flanges.

The counterweight of the lifting span was a length of iron chain of which the end rested on the mud; as the span was lowered and the strain on the guys increased, the length of the chain acting as counterweight increased. By this simple compensating device, which was designed by Col. Evans, the span could be easily lifted and lowered by two men.

One difficulty about this bridge was that it was built of hard Australian jarrah wood, no piece longer than thirteen feet and every piece warped like a corkscrew. The labour of pressing the four planks into flanges was terrific. The first layer of planks for the first flange was laid in the road by a naik. He laid the end of each plank to run straight on with the end of the last and was found looking disconsolately at a bow fifty feet long and with a seven feet bend. Every bolt was made and threaded from bar iron and every nut was made the same way. The company blacksmiths had to work day and night.

A photograph is shown in the frontispiece of this remarkable extemporisation. It continued for over a year to be the principle northern exit from the base, and though the main road now crosses the creek at Barrett Bridge constructed by No. 4 Company, King George's Own Sappers and Miners in 1916, the 22nd Company's bridge is still in constant use (1931). Also while every other important bridge in Basra is called by the name of some eminent general, this bridge still goes by the name of its builder, Whiteley's Bridge.

One of the officers of the 22nd Company (not a pre-war Sapper and Miner) who afterwards served with various R.E. field companies, writes that, at this period, 17th and 22nd Companies contained the most wonderful collection of highly skilled tradesmen he had ever seen. This was the result of the very thorough training and testing of tradesmen at Kirkee. Unfortunately in Mesopotamia, as in France, many highly skilled men were killed in action in 1914—1915 and could not be replaced. So the trades skill of the companies declined with each draft.

When the division first arrived at Basra, the climate was at its best, resembling the Punjab winter —cold nights and warm, sunny days. As the summer came on, however, the intense damp heat was very unpleasant. Mosquitoes were very bad, though this improved later when the innumerable breeding places had been filled in. An Indian N.C.O. described the Basra mosquitoes as "large as elephants and ravenous as hyenas".

The companies lived in tents. The hours of work were long—in winter while daylight lasted; in summer 5 a.m.—11 a.m. and 4 p.m.—9 p.m. There were no holidays; it was only possible to let off a section or so at a time to wash themselves and their clothes. Discipline was excellent, perhaps because no one had time for any mischief. Rations, on the whole, were good, though meat was tough and all vegetables very scarce. The men's health was very good during the winter and spring; but as the summer came on, the intense heat, long hours and lack of holidays undermind the health of all ranks and made them an easy prey to malaria.

At first the surroundings were full of interest. The troops were in a new and strange country—the country of the Thousand and One Nights. The palm trees, the appearance of the people, the shape of the boats and the general aspect of the town, which has been called the Venice of the East, all had a fascination of their own. The work was hard, but was full of interest for everyone. It was no longer a case of training work of value only as a practice—to be destroyed or dismantled immediately it was finished. Everyone felt that they were doing something worth while and contributing to the success of a wonderful adventure.

The European Club threw open its doors to all officers, and though it was a very small establishment, all obtained considerable enjoyment and a good deal of refreshment under its hospitable roof. A few Evinrude out-board motors were available and a trip up a creek whether on or off duty was a delightful experience. The local boats or bellums, which were poled against the current or rowed with it were comfortable and cheap, though the boatmen, like most town Arabs, were grasping and apt to be insolent at times. The officers would often in the evenings ride on the deserts and outskirts of Basra, exploring the paths and creeks. The chargers became quite good at crossing the water channels on very narrow planks or logs—generally it was not possible to jump them owing to the boggy state of the ground.

St. Andrew's Night, 1914, was celebrated at the R.E. Mess in great style and "Tipperary," a new and welcome importation from the Western Front—was handed out to Basra from the roof of the Turkish Admiralty House to the full capacity of a dozen lusty throats. No after effects were noticed next morning beyond a discreet grin or two amongst the sappers on parade.

As time went on and the heat replaced the pleasant winter weather and the novelty wore off, life became less interesting, and is remembered chiefly as continuous work under conditions that became increasingly dull and intolerable; but twelve months later, in view of what had happened in the interval, Basra was looked back to as a sort of Heaven.

Appendix I.

Sappers and Miners Work at Basra.

22nd NOVEMBER TO 31st DECEMBER, 1914.

Three creeks on River Road bridged for horses.
Four existing bridges repaired to take guns.
Large high and low level pier at Ordnance Depot.
  (22nd Company).
High level pier at Customs House to take guns.
Four light piers at Customs House.
Light pier and floating pier at Supply Wharf.
Work at hospital, including a light pier and a footbridge.
  (22nd Company).
Repairs to existing bridges.
Ramps for unloading horses.
Shed for ordnance stores.
Strong room for Army Pay Department.
Light suspension bridge over Ashar Creek.
Gallows in the city.
Rafts of barrels for water supply pumps.
Temporary stables for staff.
Strutted deck of S.S. Medijie to take two 18 pounder guns.
Fences for supply depot.

JANUARY, 1915.

2,000 Bangalore bombs.
Preparing barges for heavy guns.
Construction of 3 piquet posts with wire entanglement.
Temporary bridge over Khandak Creek.
Robat Bridge (8—12 foot spans, trestles and road bearers 8 inch by 2 inches timber).
Bridge over branch of Robat Creek (four spans).
Pier with barrel raft head at Headquarters.
Repairs to Customs House pier and others.

FEBRUARY, 1915.

Ashar Bridge (Whiteley's Bridge).
Flood control (Lieut. Crawford in charge).
Two piers enlarged and strengthened.
New head to hospital pier.
Second pier built alongside grass pier and the two connected by a wharf.
Bridge of two spans at Marine Barracks.
Bridge of four spans at Baghdad Gate.
Four trench mortars (wood, bound with wire).

MARCH, 1915.

Five inch gun, mounted on barge for Nakaila blockade.
Tramway from Ordnance Pier.
Air line at Gurmat Ali replaced by cable, and cable huts built.

APRIL, 1915.

(After return from Shaiba).
Piers and roadways on East bank of Shat in preparation of move to Ahwaz (12th Division).
Experiments with armoured bellums.

MAY, 1915.

Preparations for advance from Qurna.

JUNE and JULY.

Aviation barge (begun in May).
Repairs to piers.
Pile driving to protect piers.
Two double piers at Supply and Transport Yard.
Heavy piers near Turkish Hospital.
Slipway.
New pier at Customs House.
Decking barges for horses.
Pier at Post Office.
Fitting hand rails on piers.
Two bridges on Fao Road.
Assembling trusses at Aerodrome.

CHAPTER III.

Advance to Qurna.

Qurna, the traditional site of the Garden of Eden, is about 40 miles above Basra in the fork between the Tigris and the old bed of the Euphrates. It was held by about 1,200 Turkish Infantry with four guns. Part of the 18th Infantry Brigade (one Section 82nd Battery, R.F.A., one Company Norfolks, 104th Rifles and 110th Mahratta Light Infantry) under Lieut. Col. Frazer, moved against them by steamer on 3rd December. They were accompanied by the Mejidie, which had been fitted by 17th Company to take field guns, and the right half of the company with Campbell and Dunhill which embarked on the Malomar, and took with them light adjustable trestles and superstructure to make piers (Dunhill and Crawford had changed companies on 2nd December).

The force landed early on the 4th on the left bank of the Tigris, just above the inflow of the Shwaiyib, six miles south of Qurna. The Sappers made ramps for guns over two creeks, and then joined the column advancing on Mazera, following the Norfolk company at the head of the main body, carrying their tools, as no pack animals were landed. The Turks were found holding a line of trenches from the Shat-Al-Arab to Mazera. The British advance was in the direction of the village, and the 110th, which had furnished the advanced guard, attacked it. The Sappers were moved up in support of this attack and, when the Turks were driven out of the village, they came up into line between the Norfolks and the 110th, and the whole advanced through the plantations on the river bank and began to fire across the water at the Turks who had escaped across the river to Qurna and were lining the opposite bank. At 1 p.m the 104th came up on the left of the 110th and endeavoured to establish fire superiority to cover a crossing, and the Sappers were ordered to this point to assist in the operation. But this project was abandoned and the whole force fell back to bivouac near their landing place. They had inflicted severe casualties, taken 78 prisoners and two guns (which, however, could not be removed), and had lost 20 killed and 54 wounded. The Sappers had one killed and three wounded. The whole force was back at 5 p.m., after which the sappers unloaded stores and helped to dig the perimeter.

Next day (5th), the company worked strengthening the perimeter. Lt. Dunhill went out with a party to try and destroy the abandoned Turkish guns, but the Turks had recrossed the river and reoccupied their position. Lord and 10 men arrived on the 6th with material for a flying bridge. The same day, Major General Fry and the remainder of the 18th Brigade arrived. During the 6th the Sappers worked in camp making one bridge and repairing ramps. The enemy made a demonstration towards the camp but were driven back.

On the 7th the whole force attacked once more the Mazera position, which was now held by 2,000 infantry. The Sappers acted as rear-guard and took no part in the fighting, which resulted in the capture of the position and 130 prisoners. The action ended in much the same manner as that on the 4th with our troops along the left bank of the river engaged in a fire fight with the garrison of Qurna. The remainder of the enemy had retreated up stream. The force camped in the palmgroves north-west of Mazera.

It was decided to construct a flying bridge over the river one mile north of Qurna. Early on the 8th, Dunhill fetched 1,500 feet of one inch rope from the landing camp, and at 10 a.m. the company marched out to the selected point. Meanwhile the infantry were already out all along the river bank, and the Turks were shelling the camp (our casualties were two mules). Across the river, which was 130 yards wide, running fast and very cold, some mahailas were tied to the bank, but no enemy was visible. At 11.30 a.m. Havildar Gulam Nabi, Lance Naik Nur Dad and Sapper Ghulam Haider, on volunteers being called for, swam across with a log line.

They got over unmolested and were followed by Havildars Fateh Khan and Ilam Din; these five then pulled over a 1½ inch cable; Lt. Campbell followed, and a single one inch wire rope was hauled across and made fast and a mahaila hauled back to the left bank. At this point the Turks began to take an interest in the proceedings, and a desultory fire was opened from downstream but no actual attack was made on the party. On the left bank, the flying bridge tackle was rigged up. At 1.20 p.m. the first batch of 70 men of the 110th was ferried across. During the first few trips, the far end of the cable was taken down stream during the crossing to ease the strain, and taken up again with the mahaila before the return trip, but later the cable was doubled and the ends made fast to holdfasts. In this manner the whole of the 110th and one section of the mountain guns were ferried across; the Turks still only taking a moderate interest in the crossing.

The 110th advanced southwards on Qurna and were soon joined by the 104th who had seized some mahailas a few miles higher up and effected a crossing on their own. The two battalions soon found themselves up against a prepared position and the senior officer, considering there was no time to carry through an attack that evening, withdrew to the flying bridge head. The position was one of some danger as there was a considerable force of Turks on the right bank to the north. But these did not move, and during the night the Turks in Qurna, 1,100 men and four guns, surrendered.

For their gallantry on this occasion, Lieut. M. G. Gunning Campbell was awarded the Military Cross, Havildar Ghulam Nabi, Lance Naik Nur Dad and Sapper Ghulam Haidar the Indian Order of Merit, 2nd Class, and Havildar Fathe Khan the I.D.S.M.

On the 10th the company collected their kit from the landing camp and moved to Qurna. On the 11th they moved up the right bank again to just north of the flying bridge, where the brigade was now to camp. Here they remained till 5th January. On 12th December, Lord went down to Basra and returned on the 14th with the rest of the company. The work at first consisted of camp communications, and unloading facilities for river steamers.

On 15th December, the G.O.C., Poona Division, with the D.E.C., arrived at Qurna, and the latter drew up a scheme for an entrenched camp in the angle between the Tigris and Euphrates consisting of four strong points connected by trenches. The 17th Company was, during the remainder of the month, employed on this. Sniping at night by Arabs was the only interference.

On 28th December, Capt. E. J. Loring, R.E. from Kirkee, joined the company and took over the command.

On 1st January, half the company went out with a reconnaissance in force towards Muzaibila; the only work was two small bridges.

The company shifted camp back to Qurna on 5th January. At the end of December the enemy to the north had been reinforced and it was decided to increase the garrison of Qurna to two brigades. The rise of the rivers and consequent flooding had made large scale operations on the right bank of the Tigris impossible, but on the left bank the area between it and the Shwaiyib remained dry. The bulk of the garrison was therefore located at Mazera and a scheme for a defenivse position to the north and east of it, got out by the D.E.C. Major A. R. Winsloe, R.E., was put in charge of the work and the 17th Company officers, with Capt. Colbeck who had come up with the Sirmur Sappers, were in charge of various sections. The company was employed on entanglements and over-head cover along the position during the month of January and also erected a high level and a low level pier of palm log cribs no the Mazera bank and bridges on various roads. They also constructed a boom of spars across the Tigris to catch Turkish floating mines.

On 13th January, Nos. 1 and 3 Sections now moved across to camp at Mazera; the remainder stayed at Qurna.

On 20th January, the 17th Company accompanied the reconnaissance in force to the Turkish position on the Ruta Canal, seven miles north of Mazera. One section with advanced guard, and the rest with the main body.

During the retirement, the company was ordered to destroy the village of Hala, including a mud fort, with round towers, about 12 feet in diameter, at the corners. The towers came down very nicely by exploding gun cotton charges buried— frontier fashion in the floor, the curtains by undercutting with picks and pulling down, and the village huts by fire. The company had one sapper wounded during the day.

On 30th January, Lord, with a party, went out with a small force and assisted in similar demolitions at the villages of Jala and Alloa on the right bank.

On the night of 29th/30th January, some excitement was caused by a small attack by the enemy on the right of the Mazera position. They were easily repulsed, losing 46 prisoners.

On 7th February, H.E the Viceroy visited Qurna and the company had the first holiday since landing, except Christmas Day.

Early in February, the Bridging Train of the 1st K.G.O. Sappers and Miners arrived in Qurna and Campbell was placed in command. He went down to Basra to take charge in the same boat as the Turkish officer, captured in the night raid. They made friends and were delighted to find that both were very ready with their pencils and exchanged sketches. The Bridging Train erected and maintained a floating bridge of four trestles, eight mahailas and 17 pontoons between Qurna and the left bank, with a wide cut to pass the river traffic. The mahailas in the bridge cost from £200—£300 apiece. The procuring of these was no easy matter, for the Arab owners, fearing that we would seize them without compensation, fled up the creeks and Campbell had to conduct a regular cutting out expedition with armed launches to get them.

The bridge was a fine piece of work, and the operation of forming cut to let the sloops of war and other vessels pass, was very smartly done. The navy used generally to remain down stream using it as a boom against floating mines. It was hit on several occasions by Turkish shells.

In all this work, Campbell was ably assisted by Jemadar Sadar Din of the 1st K.G.O. Sappers and Miners. Campbell remained with the unit till April when, on Whiteley's death at Shaiba, he was selected by the Divisional Engineer Commander to command the 22nd Company. Capt. Sandes then took command and has recorded the subsequent adventures of the Bridging Train in his book "In Kut and Captivity".

Throughout February the 17th Company continued work on the Qurna and Mazera defences. The half company in Qurna were busy on observation posts, emplacements for searchlights, engine rooms and living rooms for searchlight detatchments, various bridges and wharves and an observation tower 100 feet high from which the Turkish camps and steamers beyond Ruta were well visable. On the Mazera side the half company was chiefly employed in wiring and overhead cover. However, on the 16th, the river rose and the area began to be flooded. All the troops were then employed on raising roads and strengthening bunds, but it was a losing fight, and on the 25th, the Shwaiyib joined forces with the Tigris and the whole area was flooded up to the trench line. It was decided to abandon Mazera except for a battalion post, and on 28th, the whole of the 17th Company was concentrated at Qurna, leaving the Sirmur Sappers to salve what was possible. The right half company moved at once to Shaiba under Loring, and the other half after completing work in hand at Qurna, moved to join them on 13th March.

CHAPTER IV.

Shaiba.

During the early part of 1915, the Turkish forces in Mespotamia were reinforced. The plan of the Turkish Commander, Suleman Askari, was to contain the British force at Qurna, to threaten our right flank by a movement through Persian Territory towards Ahwaz, but to make his main thrust straight at Basra from Nasiriyeh.

Immediately outside the palmgroves that fringe the western bank of the Shat there is a flat stretch of desert, liable to flood, and about five miles to the West a low ridge stretching from the old branch of the Euphrates to the town of Zubair. In the centre of this the British had established a post at Shaiba. In view of the reports of the Turkish concentration on the Euphrates, the 16th Infantry Brigade, under General Delamain, moved to Shaiba on 24th February, followed shortly by the 6th Cavalry Brigade. The latter on 3rd March, while carrying out a reconnaisance towards Nakaila, got involved with superior numbers of Arab and Kurd horsemen and were only saved by the presence of a company of the Dorsets from a disaster.

Matthews, with a few men of the 22nd Company, was sent to Shaiba with the 16th Brigade for water duties, but on 3rd March, on the arrival of half the 17th Company from Qurna, he was dispatched to Ahwaz for similar duties. He arrived just after the unfortunate engagement on 3rd March, when a gun was lost. The force was definitely on the defensive and Matthews was given the task of fortifying the camp with the whole brigade as his working party. This took two or three weeks to finish. Matthews did not rejoin his company till just before the advance to Amara, at the end of May.

As already stated, half the 17th Company, with Loring and Lord, reached Shaiba on 3rd March.

The area between Basra and Shaiba was already becoming flooded. The troops at Shaiba were occupying an entrenched camp and the 17th Company was busy for the next month on this. The work included headcover, machine gun emplacements, land mines, improving all the existing wire, cookhouses, latrines and dressing stations, cleaning out several wells and digging two new ones and erecting troughs.

The company was also allotted a section of the defensive line to hold in case of attack. The left half company under Dunhill arrived on the 15th March from Qurna.

Early in April news of the Turkish advance from Nasiriyeh had become more definite, the 18th Infantry Brigade was also moved to Shaiba, and the 22nd Company went there on the 7th, but by this time the desert between Basra and Shaiba had become a lake of mud and water, almost impossible to march through and not deep enough for boats, except where the 48th Pioneers were trying to cut a canal.

The British position at Shaiba consisted of an irregular horseshoe of posts and trenches as shown on Map IV.

On the 11th the enemy began to make his presence felt to the west, and on the night of 11th/12th the defences were manned, the 17th Company holding the south salient and the 22nd Company being in reserve on the right. The Turkish attack materialized about 5 a.m. from the south and south west and was supported by their artillery as soon as it was light, but our artillery soon silenced them and the attack definitely failed about 8 a.m. It was revived at 2.30 p.m. and again at dusk, continuing through the night, the Turks finally relinquishing the fight at 3.30 a.m. on the 13th.

All these attacks fell chiefly on the positions held by the 17th Company and the 48th Pioneers who had no difficulty in repulsing them by fire. With the 17th Company were some small acetylene searchlights from the Searchlight Section ; it is doubtful whether these were more efficient in attracting the enemys' fire or directing ours. The sergeant in charge, however, kept them going and was awarded a D.C.M.

During the night attack the Turks got right up to the wire in front of the 17th Company on more than one occasion. During the latter part of the night, they were heard collecting wounded men, and when day broke, several dead were found in the wire. The company lost a few wounded during the night.

During the 12th, the 22nd Company remained in the cover trench behind Kiln Post. During the night, one section occupied a front line trench south of Kiln Post. They were attacked two or three times, the enemy getting near enough for individuals to be seen, but the fire, though hot, all passed overhead.

General Melliss with the 6th Division staff (including the D.E.C.) and the 24th Punjabis got across the water to Shaiba about 8.30 p.m. on the 12th. The D.E.C's. boat was poled over by Tomlinson, his adjutant, and Sapper Nur Khan, his orderly. There was a boatman but he naturally did not care much about the job and lay down at the bottom of the boat. As they landed they came under heavy fire, either from the camp or "overs" from the Turks. Anyhow, the boatman got hit, but no one else.

On the 13th, the 16th Brigade moved out and cleared the enemy out of the ground in front of the right of our position in a very successful action, during which 400 prisoners and two guns were taken. The 22nd Company manned some of the trenches in the absence of the Infantry and a small party under Whiteley went out to demolish a tower which had been used as cover by the enemy. During the night the company again manned trenches. The 18th Brigade remained in their position, the 17th Company still in the south salient. The Turks on this flank made a somewhat feeble attack and a number dug themselves in about 500 yards from the salient. In the afternoon they tried to retire but the accurate fire of the Sappers, aided by a machine gun of the Norfolks, accounted for every man who left the trench. Eventually the surviors, five officers and about 120 men, came out and surrendered to the company. It may be noted that the 17th Company prided themselves on their musketry and had won the R.E.R.A. shield for two successive years before their mobilization.

Next morning at 9 a.m. General Melliss moved out to attack the enemy with his whole force, except the 48th Pioneers and 104th Rifles who remained to garrison the camp. The 16th Brigade (Dorsets, 117th and 120th, with 24th attached) moved off in a southerly direction, while the 18th Brigade (Norfolks, 110th and 120th) were echelonned behind the left flank. The 23rd Mountain Battery and 65th and 76th Field batteries followed the 16th Brigade. The field companies were allotted to brigades and the D.E.C. and his adjutant accompanied the divisional staff. The 22nd Company, under Whiteley and Crawford, marched behind the 117th. and the

17th Company with Loring, Lord, and Dunhill were on the extreme left rear of the 18th Brigade behind the 110th. The Sappers soon after starting, slung their rifles and carried the entrenching tools taken off the mules. The Cavalry Brigade (7th and 33rd) was on the right of the 16th Brigade.

It may not be amiss here to point out to those who ask, why Sappers were wasted in doing Infantry work. It is only necessary to say that in all such cases we were fighting against great odds and every rifle had to come into action; in the combats at Shaiba we only had some 4000 against a larger Turkish force aided by 10,000 or more Arab irregulars.

The force advanced and occupied South Mound when it became clear that the enemy was occupying a position in front of Barjasiyeh wood with his right flank west of the watch tower. General Melliss planned to attack frontally with the 16th Brigade and turn the enemy's left with the 18th, which was therefore moved across to the right rear of the 16th, the 17th Company going with them. At 11.30 the force commenced its advance against the enemy, and at about 12.20 the leading battalions, 120th and Norfolks on 18th Brigade front and 24th and Dorsets on 16th Brigade front, became hotly engaged at distances varying from 400 yards on the right to 900 yards on the left. The advance was now very difficult over the absolutely open ground. The gap between the two Brigades was very wide and about 1 p.m. the supporting battalions of the 16th Brigade 119th and half 117th (the other half was guarding the left flank) and the 22nd Company were moved into the gap. The 119th lost direction and eventually came up to reinforce the 24th and Dorsets. The 22nd Company came up on the right of the 24th and had to fill a gap of nearly 1,000 yards. The company moved with their right half company under Whiteley extended to two paces, and the left under Crawford following similarly extended.

They advanced about two hundred yards in a direction diagonal to the enemy's position and so reached the sky line of a slight undulation from which a long gentle slope ran down to the trenches. The enemy's fire became very severe, several men being hit; and Whiteley swung his half company round to face the enemy's line. Crawford's half company conforming. Whiteley then signalled the left half company to come up on his right, which it did at the double; but hardly had he done so, when the Turkish machine guns opened on the company and quickly found the range. Whiteley was hit in the chest and two other places, and men were falling rapidly. Realizing that he was in a very exposed position on a sky line, Crawford left a few men to carry Whiteley to the rear and took the rest of the company forward by rushes about a hundred yards to where another slight undulation gave some cover and a good fire position. During this advance, Subedar Firoz Ali was wounded. The company had suffered about thirty casualties in about twenty minutes, but they remained perfectly steady and full of fight.

Shortly after this, the 24th Punjabis came up on the company's left and slightly behind, and the 117th Mahrattas on the right; the latter were not visible at the time, though the 18th Brigade's firing line could be seen some distance away.

At this point, the battle became stationary in a fire fight at about 400 yards range between the entrenched Turks and the British in the open; but the 22nd Company was now in a better position and did not suffer many casualties.

On the right the 18th Brigade had similarly been brought to a standstill after deploying all its infantry but here the 17th Company received definite orders not to reinforce the firing line. They remained behind the 110th, the right battalion. However they came under considerable fire from the flanks and had a few casualties, including Loring, hit in the thigh. Later they took up a position on the right of the 23rd Mountain Battery.

At about 3 p.m. General Sir Charles Melliss, taking into consideration the bewildering mirage which made it impossible to follow events and the fact that our forward movement was checked, sent the D.E.C., Colonel Evans, back to Shaiba fort to bring out the 48th Pioneers to occupy a position to cover the withdrawal in case it became necessary to break off the fight, and also to order out all the waggons and carts available to clear the battlefield of dead and wounded.

The fire fight continued, slow progress being made and the firing line working forward to about 200 yards from the enemy's trench. The 22nd Company had fired nearly all its ammunition by 3.30. They tried to get more from the rear and failed, but eventually managed to borrow some from the 24th.

The enemy's resistance gradually weakened, and at 4 p.m. his guns ceased to fire, and both Brigades pushed forward to the trenches, which were wholly occupied by 5 p.m., a considerable number of prisoners being taken.

There remained the Turks, second position. But as preparations for attacking it were being made the enemy abandonned it and bolted. The artillery, with little ammunition left, could not do much execution and the infantry were absolutely played out. General Melliss therefore ordered a retirement as soon as the wounded had been collected. The 22nd Company retired between the 117th and 24th, and on the right the 17th Company covered the retirement of the 110th. Both companies reached Shaiba camp about 7.30 p.m.

The casualties had been :—

17th Company, Captain Loring and 6 men wounded.

22nd Company, Captain Whiteley, and 5 men killed. Subadar Firoz Ali, and 35 men wounded.

The rifle strength of this company as it marched out was 99.

Whiteley died about an hour after he had been hit; two of the men carrying him to rear were hit while doing so. He was buried in the cemetery at Shaiba.

Jemadar Mohammad Din, 17th Company, and Jemadar Ramswami Naidu 22nd Company, were awarded the I.O.M., 2nd class, for gallant conduct throughout the fighting.

The three days fighting at Shaiba was far more decisive than could be expected. The Turks had at least 7,000 regulars present and over 18,000 Arab auxiliaries, who, however, did not do much actual fighting. The Turks expected an easy victory, some officers having gone so far as to make arrangements, in advance, with certain ladies in Basra They admitted losses of 3,000 regulars on the field. The prisoners amounted to 742 and the Turks abandoned all their guns. The retreat degenerated into a rout and the Arabs turned on the Turks. The army practically ceased to exist and the Commander-in-Chief committed suicide.

On the 17th April a new position was selected at Darhamiyeh, near Zubair, as a substitute for the Shaiba camp. Here 17th Company were employed on field defences and water supply till the 29th, when they went in to Basra. 22nd Company moved to Basra on 21st April and took up their old quarters near R.E. House. Till the end of the month they were employed at the base development, work and flood defence.

Loring recovered from his wound and re-joined the 17th Company on 30th April. Campbell came from the Bridging Train to command 22nd Company, and Lieut. Garrett, I.A.R.O., was also posted to 22nd Company. Subedar Firoz Ali was invalided for his wounds, and Jemadar Ramswami Naidu promoted Subedar, and Havildar Fateh Khan (from 17th Company) Jemadar, in his place.

In the death of Whiteley, affectionately known to all his brother officers as "Bill" Whiteley, the Corps lost one of the finest young men in the Army. Physically he was a big powerful man. His personality was full of charm and every one loved him. His temper was equable and controlled. His intellect was of a high order and very few problems which came before him remained long unsolved. He had tact and a capacity of inspiring confidence in his ability in every senior officer whom it was his duty to advise and work under. When he was killed the 16th Brigade felt that they had lost a valued comrade. He was a brave man, too. Before he was called on to show his courage in the face of an enemy, General Watson, Commanding the Cavalry School where Whiteley attended as a pupil instructor, thanked the Commandant of the Corps for sending such a fine officer, and said that in dealing with young horses, Whiteley showed a rare quality of calm courage.

One day, while at the Cavalry School, Whiteley was demonstrating the felling of a tree by explosives. Having lit the safety fuze, he and the other students walked away to cover one hundred yards off. On looking round, they saw a small Indian child approaching the tree from the opposite direction to see what it was all about. Whitely knew that the fuze might burn thirty seconds more. He sprinted, "fielded" the child from underneath the tree and got clear of danger with several seconds in hand.

His influence with his Indian sappers was immense. For him they would go anywhere and do anything.

CHAPTER V.

The Advance to Amara.

On their return to Basra after the Shaiba operations, both companies were principally employed in preparing for the second battle of Qurna, better known as "Townshend's Regatta".

The country north of Qurna was flooded to a depth of about two feet, covered with reeds and intersected with deeper channels. The enemy's position consisted of two lines of redoubts on sand hills that were actually islands in the flooded area. The plan was for a brigade to advance across the flood in "bellums", the gondola-like craft of the country, covered by artillery fire ashore and from ships, while another brigade followed in paddle steamers. The island redoubts afforded ideal targets for artillery concentrations, but the scheme was nevertheless an audacious conception.

The R.E. work allotted to the two companies in the preparations was :—

One hundred shielded bellums, which were to lead the advance. Six armoured rafts for mountain guns. Twelve armoured rafts for machine guns.	22nd Company.
A barge for aeroplanes with deck overhanging 8 feet. Timber framing to allow tents to be erected on all troop barges. Cooking and sanitary arrangements to troop barges. Decking and armouring gun barges.	17th Company.

The 17th Company at first lent some men to 22nd Company to assist in cutting the steel plates for the bellums. From the 13th to the end of the month they were employed on the barges.

The 22nd Company was responsible for the fighting craft. During the early part of May, experiments were made while the company in general was employed on piers. From 7th May onwards the company was wholly employed on the armoured crafts.

Each bellum was armoured with two 6 feet by 3 feet shields, bolted together; a gap was cut in the middle to enable the centre to rest on the gunwales and the projecting pieces to reach down the water line. The shield was loopholed and erected transversely and held in position by chocks on the gunwale in front, detachable timber frames resting on the gunwale behind against more chocks and back stays of wire rope. When not required for action the shield lay on the bellums and it could be erected very quickly. The crew consisted of fourteen, four in the boat (two firing from behind the plate) and ten shoving.

Mounting a machine gun on an armoured bellum as above proved a failure. They were therefore mounted on rafts of two bellums 6 feet apart giving a 10 feet by 8 feet platform. On this, four 6 feet by 3 feet steel sheets were mounted, making a small fort (with open gorge). A false gunwale 12 inches high with a combing and breakwater fore and aft had to be added to each bellum.

The mountain gun rafts were of similar construction on a larger scale, the platform being 16 feet by 12 feet and bellums 42 feet long being used. On these two pairs of two 5 feet by $2\frac{1}{2}$ feet plates were erected as front shields, the gun firing between them, and two 6 feet by 3 feet plates as side shields.

The weather was appallingly hot; and all the cutting and drilling of the plates was by hand. The plates were cut "cold" but became so hot to handle that they had to be dropped into the water to cool off every twenty minutes. The conditions bore heavily on the older men of the company, and many collapsed, but Campbell's cheeriness and industry overcame all obstacles, and the work was finished by 24th May.

On 23rd May, Matthews got back from Ahwaz with his detachment of No. 1 Section, and on 25th May the whole company embarked for Qurna arriving at 5 p.m. next day. From the 27th—29th, they worked on final preparation of the craft for the operations. On the 30th the left half company embarked on the Blosse Lynch, while the right half company moved to Nahairat to escort howitzers.

Operations began at 5.15 a.m. on 31st. The advanced guard, 17th Brigade, covered by the artillery, pushed their bellums through the flooded reed area and by noon had occupied the Turkish first line with very little loss. It is distressing to relate that the armoured bellums on which 22nd Company had expended so much energy and ingenuity were not very successful. The resistance of the reeds against the plates, which reached the waterline on either side of the boat, was so great that progress was very slow. This had been pointed out during manufacture, and it had been suggested that the shields should not be cut so as to hang below the gunwale. But the staff decided that the plates reaching water level would enable the troops to advance safely, if slowly, against heavy fire, and that if the resistance was light, the unarmoured bellums could push on ahead. The latter is what actually happened; but it would have been impossible had not the enemy's resistance, even considering the concentrated artillery fire, been amazingly weak. During the night, the infantry actually did reverse the shields, so that the original upper edges lay flat across the gunwales.

The Sirmur Sappers accompanied the 17th Brigade in the advance, their principal duty being to detect and destroy mines. The Turks had laid mines both on land and in the river, the latter including both floating and observation mines. These were old British submarine mining gear and contained about a hundredweight of explosive, but luckily the firing equipment was defective. The Turkish engineer officer in charge, a very ancient mulazim (lieutenant) with a long white beard was taken prisoner. The naval flotilla actually anchored on top of the minefield at the end of the day.

During this day the left half company of the 22nd Company, attached to the 16th Infantry Brigade (in support) remained embarked on the Blosse Lynch. The right half company at Nahairat opened the Fort Snipe boom to allow barges and ships to pass up, and loaded the howitzers and their ammunition on barges. They returned to Qurna that night.

Early on 1st June the 17th Brigade advanced on the enemy's second position, but it was soon evident that it had been abandonned. General Sir John Nixon, the army commander, General Townshend and Captain Nunn, the Senior Naval Officer, accompanied by the D.E.C., went in a steamer to view the obstruction, composed of submerged barges, further up stream. The white bearded Turkish engineer officer was put in the bow of a boat under escort and told to point out the mines and promised that he would be shot if he made any mistake. He pointed out some near the obstruction, and Sir John Nixon, turned to the D.E.C. and said "Now, Evans, destroy those mines at once!" Having no means of doing so but his own two hands, the D.E.C. said that he wished to consult the S.N.O. These two withdrew, and, having winked at one another, returned, averring that it was not safe to deal with them till later on.

After that, Captain Nunn steamed close up to the obstruction, looked at the gap for a minute or so and said brusquely "I'm going to take the sloops through." He turned down stream to give his orders, and a detachment of the Oxford Light Infantry was embarked on H.M.S. Espiegle, the flagship, on which also were General Townshend and the D.E.C. Then the amazing pursuit began. Leading the rout was the Turkish gun boat Malamir, then some transports and lastly a helpless fleet of mahelas. The armoured tug Shaitan led the pursuit, followed by the Espiegle, another sloop and the Odin; and the Espiegle opened fire on the Turkish steamers at nine thousand yards. The extremely sinuous course of the Tigris caused the opponents as they took the bends alternately to approach and recede from one another. The last shell was fired at dusk, by which time the Malamir was on fire, the other steamers grounded, and most of the mahelas ashore. The river was full of jettisoned gear and drowning Turks; and the pursuit only ceased when the moon set and navigation was impossible.

Next day, as the sloops, owing to heavy draft, could not proceed, the S.N.O. and General Townshend and a small party of infantry continued in the Shaitan. In the early afternoon of the 3rd, the pursuit ended, when the G.O.C. and S.N.O., with an actual force of 41 ratings and other ranks, took possession af Amara and accepted the surrender of about 1,000 Turks. They maintained control till next morning, when the troops who had followed in paddle boats began to arrive.

The D.E.C. had to wait at Ezra's Tomb during the 2nd, and pushed on to Qalat Saleh next day in an old stern wheeler with some signallers. At Qalat Saleh, five wounded Germans and 200 Turks surrendered to this party. They put them in custody of the Arabs and continued their way to Amara.

The 22nd Company left Qurna in two halves at 5.30 p.m. on the 1st. They arrived at Ezra's Tomb on the second and had to spend the next day there waiting for a tow. During this day, they examined a Turkish explosive barge. The left half company under Crawford stayed there with the 17th Brigade, while the right half, with Campbell and Matthews, proceeded up river on the 4th in P. 2 (paddle steamer No. 2), salving a damaged aeroplane near Qalat Saleh on the 5th, and reached Amara at 7 p.m. on the 5th. They remained on board next day, and disembarked on the 7th, going into billets. The left half company arrived on the 10th, having found no work to do at Ezra's Tomb, where the 17th Brigade was practically on an island. The trip up the river is remembered by the Sappers as the one comfortable and pleasant experience of the whole campaign. There were good matting awnings on the boats. There was no work, no dust and no marching, while food and drink were always at hand. "We realised to the full that the Navy has a lot to be thankful for."

On June 7th, Colonel U. W. Evans, R.E., who had been D.E.C. since mobilization, was appointed G.S.O. 1 of the division. Colonel Evans as the Commanding Officer of the two companies before mobilization had an intimate knowledge of their personnel and capabilities, which had made the engineer work run with great smoothness. The end of his tenure as D.E.C. was very much regretted by all ranks, but every one was glad of his getting a good billet. He was replaced temporarily by Major A. R. Winsloe, R.E.,

Chapter VI.

Halt at Amara.

Amara is a considerable town at a point where the Tigris, after a generally easterly course, turns due south and where the Musharrah Canal, joined a few miles east of the town by the Jahala Canal, flows in from the East. The town is in the angle between the canal and the left bank of the river. The Turks had a boat bridge across the river and a trestle bridge with an archaic lifting span across the canal.

The engineer headquarters and park were fixed on the left bank, a few hundred yards below the bridge, and the 22nd Company went into billets close by. There was plenty of work for them and the Sirmur Sappers. The heat was very oppressive, though the mosquitoes were not so intolerable as at Basra. The sappers had to work long hours in the heat while the infantry were under cover, and the health of the men deteriorated rapidly, and only improved when the prospect of the advance in the autumn, combined with slightly cooler weather, came to cheer the division. The working strength of the company sometimes fell as low as thirty. The Sappers had a large gang of Arab workmen and provided them with arm bands of different colour for each trade to ensure that the right man was on the right job. Matthews encouraged them in their work with a very effective whip of rhino hide, and was on one occasion reproved by General Delamain for using it. Many months afterwards, when on the march as prisoners of war, Matthews reminded the general of this incident; on which occasion the latter reversed his previous judgment and wished that he had been able to apply the treatment to every Arab in Mesopotamia.

The following were some of the works allotted to the company :—

(1) Hangar for aeroplanes, 40 feet square by 14 feet high. This consisted of two rows of poles, at five foot intervals, which supported a taut wire net made up of binding wire. The roof and sides were covered with matting. The twisting up of the wire was very slow and monotonous in the heat and is remembered as the most tedious and trying job done by the company. Later, the wire was replaced by one inch wire rope.

(2) Improvements to hospitals, i.e., window shades, brick floors, shelves, tables and beds, cooking places. This was done by the company carpenters, assisted by Arab carpenters.

(3) Similar improvements to G.O.C's and staff quarters.

(4) Defence work; blockhouses and wire.

The blockhouses were double storied brick structures, 20 feet square, with blunted corners; loopholes were made on both floors. The upper floor, approached by wooden steps, was of brick paving on C.S.I., resting on six inch by four inch joists at two feet interval, supported by a six inch by four inch beam resting on posts. The roof was double matting on bamboo framework. There was a machicouli over the door.

(5) Four rafts to ferry guns over the river if required and a pier at which to load them.

(6) Assistance to the Bridging Train.

(7) Gun mountings for 18 pounders to go on paddle boats.

(8) Four barges prepared for four inch and five inch guns.

(9) Experiments in rafting with khufas. (These are wicker work coracles, about five feet in diameter). Work on rafts of kerosine oil tins and tarpaulins on frames. All this was in connection with crossing obstacles when the advance was resumed.

(10) Flying bridge over Jahallah Canal, with 40 feet piers on either bank, a mahaila being decked in to take guns (this was finished on 22nd July, on which day information was received that it was not wanted. The piers, however, remained and became the ends of a permanent bridge).

(11) Observation ladder for gunners on a roof. This was later developed into an observation platform.

(12) Adjustable trestles for bridging in the advance.

(13) Work on the new bridge over Tigris, done in conjunction with the Bridging Train. The company's work consisted of making trestles for the shore bays, manufacturing road bearers and decking, withdrawing and refitting groups of boats and replacing them in bridge with the new material.

(14) Fitting a barge for five inch guns. This consisted of decking two lengths of 45 feet with double decking rested on rafters, supported by saddles on the gunwales and down the centre; armoured protection was fixed for the guns.

(15) Two barges decked for horses.

(16) Caulking bellums.

(17) Masts for wireless aerials on ships.

(18) Ramps for landing field guns and horses from barges.

The cavalry and infantry ramps were pairs of two feet wide roadways resting on a trestle with hinged struts. It could be put up in a few minutes. The artillery ramps were similar but of heavier construction and fitted with inner and outer wheel-guides; the trestles were made with adjustable transoms to make a ramp up (or down) to any probable height of bank.

(19) Camouflaging the Blosse Lynch to give her the appearance of a cruiser. This was done by erecting a second mast, a third (canvas) funnel, fighting tops of canvas on the masts and mounting four canvas guns in galvanized iron turrets.

On 10th June, Crawford and 20 men proceeded by boat down the Jahalah Canal to bridge three canals on the left bank, to facilitate the march in of the 12th Brigade, which had been operating from Ahwaz.

Crawford went sick on completion, and, on the 13th Matthews relieved him and constructed six bellum rafts to convey guns and waggons over the marshes; on the way back, Matthews had to help the gunners a good deal and retrieve two of their waggons from the canal.

On 24th June, Campbell carried out a reconnaissance along the left bank of the Tigris as far as the Bitairah Canal.

On 28th June, Matthews and Garrett and No. 1 Section went with the 22nd Punjabis to Kumait, 20 miles up the Tigris, where an advanced post was to be established. The work here was mostly wiring the post and water supply; Matthews came back on 12th July.

On 30th July, Crawford and No. 2 Section sailed in a barge up the river, loaded with wire, sandbags, rafting and bridging materials, etc. They picked up Garrett and No. 1 Section at Kumait and went on to Ali Gharbi with the 16th Brigade. Here they stayed six weeks, making piers, shoring up buildings and fortifying a small post, to be occupied by half a battalion and two 15 pounders. Another task was the manufacture of hand grenades and the instruction of the infantry in their use. Eventually, the chief interest became the maintenance of the river side road; this mostly slipped into the river under military traffic, and in places the outer edge had to be supported on timber girders, resting on piles and trestles. The half company remained at Ali Gharbi till Campbell and the left half company picked them up on 11th September.

Jemadar Chowharja Baksh Singh, who had come out to Basra with a draft in May, joined 22nd Company in Amara, but he was transferred to 17th Company on 1st July, vice Jamadar Ganpatrao Jadhao, who had long been ill, and was eventually invalided to India on 24th July.

CHAPTER VII.

Nasiriyeh.

We must now revert to the 17th Company, left at Basra when the advance from Qurna began. General Townshend tried to get them back to his division but failed. They remained at the base working at its development.

However, a change was in store for them. It was decided that, before any advance from Amara could be made, it was necessary to occupy Nasiriyeh, on the Euphrates, some 70 miles west of Qurna, which had served as advanced base for the Turkish Army that had been defeated at Shaiba. For this purpose, Major General Gorringe with the 30th Brigade and some divisional troops, including 12th Field Company, 2nd Queen Victoria's Own Sappers and Miners, moved off from Basra on 30th June. This detachment forced its way across the Hammar lake and through the Akaika channel to the Euphrates, some 20 miles below Nasiriyeh but found themselves held up by Turkish positions on both banks between the river and the marshes. The 12th Brigade was sent up as reinforcements but proved insufficient. The 18th Brigade from the 6th Division was therefore sent up, and on 16th July, the 17th Company received orders to embark an for unknown destination without their mules. They embarked at 4 p.m., arrived at Qurna next day, and at Asani Camp on the 20th at 3 p.m.

Like all river journeys, this trip was a pleasent interlude. The only incident was that the company had to tow the steamer and its barges though the cut in the Akaika dam—four ropes for each vessel.

No 1 Section was left in camp with Lord; the remainder moved up the right bank of the river to join the 30th Brigade, ('1/4th Hampshires, 24th and 76th Punjabies, and 2/7th Gurkha Rifles) who were holding a position—Sixteen Palms-Shukhair—

about two miles above the camp. Here for the next two nights the company worked on the position. On the 23rd the company collected and loaded bridging material in an iron barge for the next day's operations.

The Turks, in strength 4,000, with 15 guns, were holding both banks of the river about seven miles below the town. On the left bank the attack was to be made by the 12th Brigade, and on the right by the 30th, the 18th Brigade being in reserve. The Turks on the right bank were in trenches about 700 yards from ours, and about 150 yards from their front line ran the Majanina Creek, 60 feet wide, and believed unfordable. The plan was that the 17th Company and a company of the 48th Pioneers (40 strong) should bridge this creek to allow the infantry to assault. No reconnaissance was made for the bridge as the operation was to be a surprise.

At 5.30 a.m., the West Kents opened the attack on the left bank in great style, and by 6.40 a.m. the 12th Brigade had carried the advanced Turkish trench system on the left bank. The 17th Company and 40 men of the 48th Pioneers under Captain Hewett, and a covering party 30 strong of the Hamshires were in the bridging barge, which was towed by the Sumana. As soon as it was seen that the 12th Brigade attack had succeeded, the Sumana and her tow moved up river, covered by three river steamers. Naturally every available Turkish gun and rifleman opened on them, and both vessels were knocked about a good deal, but the Sumana pushed her barge into the creek mouth at about 7.30 a.m., and the bridging parties leapt into the water. Lord and some of the sappers jammed the barge across the creek, and the remainder threw the bridging material overboard. Here the bank gave the sappers cover, and the Hampshire detachment lined the far bank against counter attack. In about an hour three bridges were across. Trestles had been made beforehand and the road bearers prepared for fixing, but Sapper Hari Tingre, who had been taught the correct way to lay chesses and saw no reason for it being done otherwise, got up on the road bearers and put on the planks in the approved manner fully exposed to to the enemy's close range rifle fire. By some astounding chance he was only wounded once and completed the job to his satisfaction before coming down.

Jemadar Mohammad Din was also conspicuous, as always, for gallantry and entire disregard of danger.

The bridging, which was finished by 8.30 a.m., was not completed without loss. Jemadar Chowharja Baksh Singh was killed by a bullet through the head while speaking to Loring about the roadway of the central bridge. Lord was shot through the leg while completing the unloading of the barge. Loring, and Sergts. Toleman and Baker were slightly wounded, and fifteen Indian other ranks were wounded.

When the bridges had been completed there ensued a long wait. About 9.30 a.m., assaulting infantry (Hampshires and 2/7th Gurkhas) arrived on the near bank. But a change had taken place. The Euphrates creeks flow out of, not into the river: the barge had dammed the flow and the creek, which had been five feet deep, was now easily fordable. The infantry did not use the bridges, but were partly carried, partly helped, across by the Sappers and Pioneers. At 9.40 a.m., the assault went forward from the far bank and the Turks bolted, leaving five field guns and one hundred prisoners.

After the assault the distance of the bridges from the trenches was paced; it was 148 yards.

The Turks still had a reserve position, but when in the afternoon the British advanced on both banks, they again retreated and evacuated Nasiriyeh in the night. The town was occupied next day, the 25th, and this ended the operations in which the Turks lost all their guns and half their strength in killed, wounded and prisoners.

After the creek position had been carried, the 17th Company advanced behind the infantry and spent the rest of the day collecting the enemy's arms and ammunition. They passed the night on the battlefield. They continued the collection next day, and in the evening embarked and were towed up to Nasiriyeh.

The strength of the company on the 24th was fifty five. The company was thanked by the G.O.C., 12th Division, and the G.O.C., 30th Brigade, for their services, the former (General Gorringe) walking two miles in the heat of the day to make the men a speech and compliment them on their exploit.

On the 26th they went back to Asani, where they fitted up a barge for use as a hospital and collected and loaded up all R.E. stores in camp or on the battlefield. On the 29th, this being completed, they were towed up to Nasiriyeh again and pitched camp there. Here they stayed till 6th August, decking mahailas and constructing small bridges and making bricks for

---

FOOTNOTE. The official History gives different timings for this operation and states that the assaulting Infantry reached the creek before the barge. The account given here is, however, believed to be correct.

a model barrack hut which they actually started to build. On the 6th however, the 18th Brigade and other 6th Division troops having already gone, the company embarked on the barge, went off down steam, arriving at Basra on the 10th. Here they spent a week, chiefly decking barges, and at 3 p.m. on the 16th left Basra for the last time on " P.I.," which after breaking down once or twice delivered them to their own division at Amara on the 20th August. Lord was invalided back to India with his wound, which left him permanently lame. Havildar Gangajirao Khanwilkar was promoted Jemadar, vice Chowharja Baksh Singh.

For the Nasiriyeh operations Loring and Lord both received the Military Cross, and Sapper Hari Tingre the Indian Order of Merit, second class.

At Amara the company stayed till 10th September. During these three weeks, the men were employed, like 22nd Company, on piers and bridges in the town and preparations for the advance. The latter included making frames to hold canvas water tanks on transport carts and making up "Wheatly bag" bridges, the predecessor of our present kapok floating bridges The 17th Company was billetted half a mile up stream from the 22nd Company, but the two units saw a lot of one another again. On the 10th September the company moved by water to Ali Ghabi. On this day also, Lieuts. A. T. East and W. R. Boyes, I.A.R.O., joined. This marked the beginning of a new phase. The officers now with the companies were:—

17th COMPANY.	22nd COMPANY.
Capt. E. J. Loring.	Capt. M. G. G. Campbell.
,, C. M. G. Dunhill.	,, A. B. Matthews.
Lieut. A. T. East.	,, K. B. S. Crawford.
,, W. R. Boyes.	Lieut. Garrett.
Sub. Baryam Singh.	Sub. Ramswami Naidu.
Jem. Mohammad Din.	Jem. Tek Singh.
,, Gangajirao Khanvilkar,	,, Fateh Khan.
Sergt. Toleman.	Sergt. Bellis.
,, Baker.	

CHAPTER VIII.

Kut-Al-Amara 1915. (Es-Sinn).

The forward concentration for the advance on Kut began on 1st September. The right half of 22nd Company with Crawford and Garrett, was already there with the 16th Brigade. The remainder of the two companies arrived on 11th September.

For the operations, the 6th Division had been divided by Maj. Gen. Townshend into two columns: Column A under Maj. Gen. Delamain, 16th and 17th Brigades with attached troops; two battalions of the 30th Brigade were added later; Column B, 18th Brigade with attached troops. 22nd Company were attached to column A, and 17th Company to Column B.

The left half of 22nd Company moved by river (S.S. Julnar) and the remainder of the two companies marched, improving the roads on the way. Shaikh Saad was reached on the 14th and Sunnaiyat on the 16th.

On the 14th, Campbell and seven men of 22nd Company loaded 200lbs. dynamite on the Blosse Lynch and on the 15th proceeded with a naval escort and a party of the Norfolks to try and destroy the boom near Kut; but the enemy's fire on the bank was too strong for the ships to pass. The companies remained at Sunnaiyat till the 25th, the camp of the force being on the right bank, not on the site of the fighting of 1916-17. The 22nd Company built a 30 foot observation tower on arrival, and both companies had work on camp defences, communications and water supply. On the 19th, the pontoon and boat bridge arrived from Ali Gharbi and both companies, working by reliefs, assisted the Bridging Train to put it across the river, the 280 yard bridge being completed in six hours. Two portable observation towers were also made and 70 seven foot bamboo ladders to assist in assaults across wire. These ladders appear never to have been used. The

Turkish obstacles consisted of very inferior wire and staked military pits.

The Turkish position covering Kut was astride the river. On the right bank, it extended five miles southwards along the Essinn Banks (an old canal) to the Dujailah Redoubt. This was the position which the relief force failed to capture on 8th March, 1916. On the left bank, it extended seven miles and was broken into three separate systems by the Horseshoe and Suwada marshes; the left flank, originally rested on the Ataba marsh which, however, had receded about 2,000 yards from it. Two miles east of the Ataba marsh lay the extensive Suwaikiya marsh. Five miles west of the position, the Turks had a bridge of boats, where the general reserve was stationed. The trenches were well designed and dug.

Gen. Townshend's plan was as follows :—

Column B was to contain the enemy between the Suwada and the river; Column A was to advance up the right bank to deceive the enemy, and then, leaving only a skeleton force on that bank, to move by night to the enemy's extreme left flank for the decisive attack.

Column B was to conduct the pursuit by river, and the 17th Company loaded up their kits in S.S. Julnar on the 25th in anticipation.

The force advanced to Nakhailat on the 26th; Crawford and No. 1 Section marched with the advanced guard of Column A, on the right bank. The remainder of the two companies (except 22nd's baggage) moved by steamer. The whole of the sappers landed on the left bank below Nukhailat. The 22nd Company erected their two portable observatories and the 17th Company erected a platform 27 feet high for the army staff. There was some artillery fire in the evening and C.S.M. Bellis, 22nd Company, was wounded. During the night the 18th Brigade (Column B), took up a position of readiness opposite the Turkish trenches on either side of the Horseshoe marsh. Dunhill and the right half of 17th Company, were out to assist them.

The Bridging Train had towed up the bridge from Sunnaiyat in sections and had put it across the river at Nukhailat by 4 p.m.

The 17th Company observation tower was principally used during the action by Gen. Townshend and his staff, but Sir John Nixon mounted it once or twice. The portable observatories, which were intended for brigades, were used by the artillery.

Column A, remained on the right bank on the 27th, and made a feint of attacking the Turks opposite them.

Column B, (18th Brigade) advanced during the morning on the left bank and by the afternoon had established itself within 2,000 yards of the enemy. Dunhill's half company worked with them. The other (left) half company of 17th Company was taken out of Column B into divisional reserve and spent the day improving the track northward from the bridge.

During the 27th, 22nd Company did some repairs to the bridge, made a third observation post and wired a bridge head post on the right bank. At 5.15 p.m., they marched to join Column A as it crossed the bridge, and continued with them, doing some road work on the way to Clery's post (established by the flank guard during the march on the 26th) at the south east corner of the Suwada marsh at 7 p.m. where the column bivouacked.

Gen. Delamain had divided Column A into two portions; Brigadier Gen. Hoghton with his (17th) Brigade and the 104th and 20th from the 16th Brigade, was to attack the enemy's left flank from the left, while the Dorsets, 117th and the 22nd Company were to attack the left flank from the front. Column A, moved off, guided by Matthews, * Hoghton's echelon in front, while 22nd Company marched at the head of Delamain's echelon. Matthews led the force accurately to the south west corner of the Suwaikiya marsh, where Delamain's echelon deployed in the half light about 5 a.m. Delamain's intention was that the cavalry brigade should march between the Ataba and Suwaikiya marshes and that Gen. Hoghton should work round between the extreme left of the Turks and the Ataba, but Hoghton actually followed the cavalry and marched round the Ataba marsh. This delayed Delamain's plans to some extent. He advanced slowly towards Northern Redoubt, 117th in front with 22nd Company and Dorsets in support. At 8 a.m. this force was about 2,000 yards north east of Northern Redoubt.

At 8.45 a.m., 22nd Company received orders to come up on the 117th's right and the two units carried the attack forward opposite Northern Redoubt and the trenches opposite it. The right half company was in front, extended to about four paces, No. 1 Section under Crawford on the right, and No. 2 Section under Matthews on the left, where the company merged

---
* Captain Matthews' account of the reconnaissance for and guiding of this night march is given as an appendix to this chapter.

into the 117th. There was none of the pace and excitement of Sahil, and the fire was much heavier; there was no cover but the men pushed on steadily. Subadar Ramswami Naidu was killed early in the advance. When the line had got to 350 yards from the trenches, half the Dorsets came up to reinforce, and the left half of the 22nd Company, which had been in support, came into the firing line. The advance continued and at 10 a.m., the remainder of the Dorsets came up and three units charged in together. The Turkish wire consisted of a few strands only and did not check the Sappers. As they reached the parapet, the Turks surrendered, the few who resisted being bayonetted (Sapper Sohan Singh got three). Crawford was the first man to reach the parapet.

Almost at the same time, Hoghton's echelon coming down the west side of the Ataba marsh, struck the left rear of the enemy's position.

The two brigades now worked down the position slowly driving the Turks out of the system. At 12.45 Southern Redoubt was captured. During this period 22nd Company acted as escort to the artillery and came under intermittent artillery fire only. Hoghton pushed on to a point west of the Suwada marsh, but his men were about played out and he retired towards the marsh to try and get some water. Delamain joined him here, having completed the clearing up of the trench system.

Meanwhile, the cavalry brigade had worked round on to the Turkish rear, near their boat bridge but they failed to hold their position. Column B, under Gen. Fry, on the left, worked forward very deliberately towards the positions near the Horseshoe Marsh. By 4.30 p.m. the 18th Brigade line was about 900 yards from the trenches.

About 4.50 p.m., Delamain, having rested his men, got Column A into motion again. 17th Brigade leading and 18th Brigade echeloned on the right rear, the 22nd Company and the guns following 17th Brigade. By 5.30 p.m., he had got on to the rear of the Horseshoe position, and was about to attack it, when a large Turkish force, from the right bank, suddenly appeared advancing from his right. The two brigades wheeled into line and drove them off in most gallant fashion, our men following them up till darkness rendered pursuit impossible. But by this time the men were absolutely played out and the force settled down for the night where they stood. The 22nd

Company, still escorting the guns, joined them at 9. p.m. The temperature dropped to $50°$ F and the men who had been suffering from thirst and heat all day, now suffered from cold. At 4 a.m. on the 29th, the company stood to arms.

Meanwhile Column B. (18th Brigade) were unable to get much nearer the enemy, and they finally dug themselves in about 500 yards from the trenches. The Cavalry Brigade lost itself trying to find water. The net had nearly closed round the Turkish left wing, but not quite. They made a successful escape in the dark.

The 17th Company spent the day half in divisional reserve and half with 18th Brigade reserve.

At 8 a.m. on the 29th Column A, finding no enemy about, marched to the river. The men had had no meal since the start of the night march on the 27th and no water except that in water bottles and pakhals. The 22nd Company was well up during the march to the river, and on reaching the bank, had to right wheel and march along it till the rear troops got to the water. As soon as the column halted every man walked into the river up to his waist and drank till he could drink no more.

At noon on the 29th the 16th Brigade marched into Kut, 22nd Company in the vanguard on road work, and bivouacked outside the town. The 2nd line transport rejoined the company at 5.15 p.m.

An attempt at pursuit had commenced on the night of 28th/29th, when Commander Cookson, R.N., of the Comet, was killed in trying to break through the Turkish boom. The latter was actually passed at 10 a.m. on the 29th, but the low state of the river hampered the gunboats and the pursuit was never effective.

The Cavalry did overtake the Turks but could not interfere with them.

The 18th Brigade embarked above the obstruction. Here the 17th Company had to help to get the guns on board and also exploded several Turkish mines. In the evening the right half company, under Dunhill, marched into Kut to join Column A. (16th Brigade).

The left half company, with Loring, embarked on the Julnar in the evening, and till 5th October they moved up the river sticking frequently on the way; on the 5th, the Column arrived at Aziziyah, 60 miles above Kut.

The Turks lost about 4,000 men at the battle of Essinn, leaving 14 guns and 1,150 prisoners in our hands. The British losses were 1,233.

The company's losses on the 28th were :—

Subedar Ramswami Naidu, I.O.M. and Havaldar Jawahir Singh killed: Jamadar Tek Singh and 18 I.O.R. wounded.

Subedar Ramswami Naidu was a remarkable example of a very old sapper conviction, dating from the time of Broadwood, that men of all types and races will make fine soldiers if properly handled. The subedar was a Telugu, a man of an unwarlike race, but he was a fine Indian Officer with plenty of brains and "guts." He commanded the respect and willing obedience of the whole company. He was incidentally a very fine rifle shot.

As a consequence of the casualties in 22nd Company, Jemadar Muhammad Din, I.O.M., from 17th Company, was transferred as a Subedar, and Colour Havildar Krishna Bhonsle promoted Jemadar in 17th Company in his place. Havildar Major Shankaram Pille was promoted Jemadar in 22nd Company vice Tek Singh. The latter was invalided to India in December from his wounds.

Appendix II.

Captain Matthews' account of the night march round the marshes.

Two days before we marched, I was told that there would be a night march soon in a rough north westerly direction, and that I would have to lead it. I talked it over with Campbell and suggested that the best way to do it was by the stars and that it would be better to take bearings on stars for the next two nights and so not have to rely on a compass. So the next two nights I spent taking bearings and plotting them out for every hour.

On the morning of the day, I was given an æroplane sketch and shown exactly where to go, but on the sketch was marked; "rough sketch bearings not accurate". I suggested that I had better take a few men and ride out and find the edges of the swamps so as to be sure that we would skate round them and not into them. However, I was told that on no account was any man allowed to be seen out on that flank. After a lot of trouble we got an æroplane to go up. He was to go to the north and fly right over certain selected points, the edges of marshes and the end of the trench we were to attack. These points were numbered on his sketch and on mine and over each point, in order, he was to do a dip and I was to follow him with a prismatic and take bearings from the starting point of the march to his dips. He only got up an hour or so before dark and added some element of doubt to the whole thing by making some of the bearings more than 10 degrees out with the sketch, some one way out and some others. Probably this was caused by the wind blowing the marsh swamps about. By the time I got back and showed the "revised" sketch to Delamain it was dark. He seemed pretty worried about it and so was I, since it is not easy to take a bearing with accuracy on to a rather vague "dip" done a long way off by a plane. Delamain took me along to see

Townshend on his ship and by this time the march to the starting point had started. I think Delamain, although he didn't say so, was for waiting a day and having a recheck on bearings. Townshend was singularly unimpressed. "Ten degreess make no difference one way or another to the soundness of my plan" were his actual words. Nor it would if there had been any definite land marks of any sort to march for, or if there had been any hope that the actual enemy's position would be visible from where the column should be at day break. Having seen the unrelaibility of bearings there was the knowledge that distances would also be wrong.

Off we gaily went. No compass was used at all. The actual keeping direction was easy, but the feeling that one had no certainty as to where the cursed marsh would be was not so good. I was in a funk that we might hit a rentrant in the swamps and felt so uncertain of the map that I would not have known then if I had hit the inner or the outer swamp and would have been properly lost. The course was set to clear them all well and it did. As far as distance went it was also a bit trying. After I had gone a certain number of paces I sent word to Delamain that as far as I knew we were then on the spot marked on the map, but since it was all dead flat desert there was no possible way of knowing. I went and saw him and told him that the end of the trench line was at that moment directly under a certain star and that half an hour before drawn it would be under another star. That finished it as far as I was concerned. I didn't hand over to Hoghton personally. Probably there was some mix up in fixing his position on his map or in giving him his direction. As a matter of fact I found out next day that the trench actually was under the proper star. This was a most unpleasant night march and I learnt many things by it and resolved if ever I had to do another that I would get a good deal of assistance and would just wander along myself with very little to worry about.

CHAPTER IX.

Halt at Aziziyah and advance to Ctesiphon.

The 22nd Company remained in Kut till 5th October. From the 1st, they were in camp on the left bank north of Kut. The work done was chiefly on roads, including bridges over several small raised irrigation channels. An enclosure, two hundred yards square, was also wired for prisoners. Garrett and a party also spent from 2nd to 4th on the battlefield with 17th Brigade, exploding mines and dismantling I.C. engines.

On the 6th, 22nd Company commenced the march to Aziziyah with the 17th Brigade. The Sappers marched with the advanced guard and had a certain amount of road making to do. Marches were begun at 5.30, or 6 a.m., and a halt made from 10 a.m. to 4.30 p.m., when the march was resumed till 9 p.m. Aziziyah was reached at 10 a.m. on the 9th and immediately the company got to work on camp communications.

The two companies remained at Aziziyah till the middle of November. The whole division had concentrated there on the 11th. The troops dug in the tents for warmth and as a protection against the continual night sniping. The principal work done was:—

17th Company

Flying Bridge and foot bridge across the Tigris. The company commenced a foot bridge of Wheatly bags on 7th October, but the current was too strong. A flying bridge with Wheatly bag raft, to take a field gun, was therefore erected instead. Later the bridging train completed a Wheatly bag foot bridge, but on the arrival of their pontoons on the 17th October, they constructed a normal bridge, assisted by part of 22nd Company.

Wiring posts for the entrenched camp (the Army Commander objected to the amount of wire used).

Wells near the river bank, revetted with brushwood gabions. These turned out to be salt.

Observation towers.

Mining a mound used by the Turks for an observation post.

22nd Company.

Mobile observatory for G.O.C.

Other observation posts and dugouts.

Lots of wiring.

Assisting Bridging Train on 17th October.

Wiring burial ground.

Both companies were also employed on making and laying sundried bricks of which large numbers were required for blockhouses, as it was expected that Aziziyah would become an important post on the L. of C. A large brickyard was established on the river bank. Loop hole plates were also made up.

On 26th October, large reinforcement drafts arrived. During 1914-15, Mussalman recruiting had been very brisk, and that of Sikhs very difficult owing to the very heavy demands on the latter community. Both companies now were re-organized with two Mussalman Sections, one Mahratta and one Sikh and mixed Hindu.

On the night of 27th/28th an operation was undertaken to try and mop up a small Turkish force at Kutuniyeh, 8 miles away, and also to blood the reinforcements that had reached all units. Both companies went out, 17th Company, with the exception of a small party with the G.O.C's. observatory, doing escort to the ammunition. The 22nd Company had its right half under Matthews attached to 18th Brigade and left under Campbell to 16th Brigade, both marching with the advanced guards. A very accurate night march was made but the Turks got away in time to avoid being cut off. The recruits, however, managed to get off their rifles at hostile Arabs and the company demolished the fort at Kutuniyeh with picks and explosives.

On 31st October and 1st November the right half of the 17th Company went out for some operations with 17th Brigade, being chiefly employed on road making.

The stay at Aziziyah is remembered as the easiest time that the Sappers had in Mesopotamia. It was getting cooler and the men began to pick up a lot. There were a good number of sandgrouse and bustard in the desert which afforded a change of rations to the officers, though, owing to shortage of cartridges, unorthodox methods of securing them were employed, the bag per cartridge being high. Morale was very high and people even began to be sorry for the Turks in view of the tremendous clouting they were going to receive when the advance was resumed.

On 11th November, the Cavalry Brigade and the 18th Infantry Brigade advanced to Kutuniyeh. The concentration of the division there was finished on the 18th. The boat bridge was moved up to Kutuniyeh on the 16th and one section of 17th Company under Boyes helped with its erection.

On the 18th, the 17th Brigade, with the 17th Company, crossed to the right bank and the bridge was dismantled. On news being received, however, that the Turks were advancing it was hurriedly reformed and the 17th Brigade entrenched on their bank. (Boyes, and his section helped in all this bridging). The next day, however, the rest of the division advanced to Zor, the 17th Brigade and the bridge following them and arriving at 9 p.m. East, with No. 1 Section. 17th Company, was now attached to the Bridging Train instead of Boyes and remained with them till their arrival in Kut in December. Next morning the bridge was again erected, the brigade crossed over and followed the rest of the division to Lajj, where the boat bridge was again put up.

When the advance from Aziziyah was commenced on 11th November the chief problem for the Sappers was the transport of engineer materials. The bulk of these materials was of course transported by water, but as it was never certain at that time of year whether the steamers and barges would reach a given place, at a given time, owing to the large number of sand banks, it was necessary to carry a proportion of all stores, including timber, by land. The extra transport allotted for this purpose consisted partly of carts and partly of camels. The carts came from the Jaipur Transport Company, each drawn by a pair of ponies (entire) and camels were recruited locally with one Arab driver to half a dozen or more camels. A great deal of trouble was experienced at first with both these forms of transport : the ponies were getting bigger feeds than they had been brought up on and the camels, bewildered by the earnest efforts of the Sappers who were not experienced at loading them, would rush straight off into the desert shedding a large part of their loads, sometimes a good distance from the camp. After the first few days the transport steadied down a bit and, though the camel is always in a vile temper for the first hour of his working day, there is no doubt that taking him all round he is the finest and most reliable form of animal transport in a desert country ; the camels always arrived in camp far ahead of the troops instead of far behind, never showed any signs of fatigue and never seemed to suffer any casualties. Their rationing was exceedingly simple as they lived chiefly on the dry camel thorn alongside the river. We put five maunds on a camel but the Arab and Turks put a great deal more, sometimes double. The drawback to the ponies was their unsteadiness at nullah crossings and in deep sand. The Indian "drabi" did magnificent work in Mesopotamia, as did the army mules.

Work on the march consisted chiefly of helping Sandes with his boat bridge, when urgency required it, and preparing nullah crossings. Brigade headquarters usually marched at the head of the brigade, accompanied by a R.E. officer and followed immediately by a half company of Sappers. Some of the nullahs were 30 feet deep.

The Turkish position at Ctesiphon, about 32 miles distant by land from Aziziyah and six from Lajj, was astride the river which flows in huge loops in a general west-south-west direction between these places. The position lay partly on the right bank where it was held by the 35th Division ; on the left bank the first line extended for six miles in a north-north-east direction and consisted of 15 redoubts connected by fire trenches. The southern half of the line from the river to the High Wall (an ancient L. shaped enbankment), where the road crossed the position, lay behind a bend in the Tigris. The extreme left of this line rested on two redoubts on low mounds, which were called the Vital Point or V.P. by General Townshend. The northern half of the line was wired and well organized with communication trenches back to reserve positions.

A second line of defence, much less prepared, lay about 4,000 yards to the left rear. The arch of Ctesiphon lay about 500 yards from the river, half way between the two lines. A third line existed behind the Diyalah river which flows into the Tigris from the north, 10 miles north-west of Ctesiphon. The Turks had a boat bridge across the Tigris behind the second line.

It had taken six months to prepare this position under German supervision; the trace was remarkably good and the flanking arrangements excellent ; the trenches were very deep and all the excavated earth was scattered.

The right half of the Turkish position on the left bank was held by the 38th Division, and the left half by the 45th Division. The 51st Division was in general reserve in the second line on the left bank. The 51st Division were Anatolian Turks, the best fighting material in the Ottoman Empire. The 45th Division was also good, but the 35th and 38th were Arabs and poor material.

The Turks also had a cavalry brigade on their extreme left rear.

CHAPTER X.

Ctesiphon.

On the night of 21st/22nd November, General Townshend moved against the Turkish position in four columns,

Column C, under Brigadier General Hoghton, consisting of the 17th Infantry Brigade and attached troops, including the 17th Company, was to make a holding attack on the left centre of the enemy's position on either side of the Water Redoubt from a point two miles north-east of Bustan. This attack was to become decisive as soon as the brigade commander saw Column A advancing.

The remaining three columns were to move to a position opposite the enemy's left flank, Column A, under Maj. Gen. Delamain, consisting of the 16th and 30th Brigades, (six battalions) and attached troops, including the right half of 22nd Company under Campbell, were to move to a position 5,000 yards east of "Vital Point". Column B, under Brigadier Gen. Hamilton, consisting of the 18th Infantry Brigade and attached troops, including the right half of 22nd Company under Crawford, were to move to a point three miles north-east of this; and the Flying Column, under Major General Mellis, V.C., (Cavalry Brigade and 76th Punjabis in carts) two miles further on. The plan was that the two latter columns were to turn the Turkish left and cut their communications while Delamain smashed the Vital Point.

These three columns moved off at 7.30 p.m., on the 21st; led by Matthews, who had made observations of the stars the previous two nights and used them entirely. An Infantry officer checked by compass, but Matthews had no difficulty in bringing the troops to their allotted positions, Column A at midnight; Column B about 1 a.m., and the Flying Column at 3 a.m.

The guiding was comparatively easy as the old Nahrwan

canal afforded a land mark, but, after his experience at Es-Sinn, Matthews was taking no risks. He had taken observations of the stars the two previous nights. For the march he was assisted by Captain Morland and three other officers and four men of the Oxford Light Infantry and he arranged them as follows :—

| B.O. | Distance | Capt. | Distance | B.O. |
| (Direction) | Party. | Matthews. | Party. | (Direction). |

< 50 yards × 50 yards >

<   200 yards   ×   200 yards   >

The distance parties each consisted of a British officer and two other ranks. The latter counted paces and after every hundred nudged the British officer, who had only to count the hundreds.

The two direction finding officers, of whom Morland was one, were given a compass bearing, and were also shown a star that was " on ". They then walked out 200 yards from the centre and marched for half an hour on their star or bearing. At the end of the half hour they marched in on Matthews, counting steps, and the centre was found. They were then given a fresh star and the process repeated. The direction was never more than fifty yards out. The distance checking was not nearly as accurate.

This method relieved Matthews of all minor worries. All five officers knew the course set and all the distances: so that had one or more parties run into Arabs and become casualties, the column would still probably have reached its destination. The direction parties were placed well out so as to have no one close enough to deflect them. The halts to check direction were not felt by the main body.

At first there was a lot of drifting cloud, which made indentification of stars difficult, but after the first half hour there was no difficulty. Column A was dropped in its proper place at midnight and Column B at 1 a.m. Matthews then told the Flying Column where it was and how far along the ancient canal banks its proper place was. It proceeded there, arriving at 3 a.m., and Matthews rejoined his half company with Column B.

Column C moved out of camp about 2.30 p.m.

Previous to marching out, the 17th Company was divided into three groups, No. 3 Section under Boyes, marched with the five inch guns and No. 1 Section, under East, was with the Bridging Train. The remainder of the company, with Loring and Dunhill, marched with the advanced guard. The column rested and watered on the river bank about four miles out and moved off about 5.30 p.m. Thereafter one section moved with the 76th Battery, R.F.A., making a road for them, while the other section made a parallel road for the transport. The assembly position was reached at midnight and the two sections reunited and the men rested as well as the bitter cold would permit.

The advance was resumed at dawn (about 6 a.m.) The front line consisted of the Oxfords on the right and the 119th and the support line of 22nd and 48th Pioneers, less one company guarding our one surviving aeroplane which had developed troubles and come down. The half 17th Company followed the 22nd Punjabis. The direction of the advance was towards the Ctesiphon Arch, i.e., to the left of that intended.

The Turks reserved their fire and the 17th Brigade pushed slowly forward. At 8 a.m. they were within 2,000 yards of the trenches and halted for reconnaissance.

At 9 a.m. the advance was resumed and when the foremost lines were about 1,000 yards from the enemy, the latter opened a heavy fire with machine guns and musketry. By 10.30 a.m. the 17th Brigade had got within 700 yards of the enemy, the supports still unused.

Boyes and No. 3 Section had considerable work in getting the five inch guns across nalas. On arrival at the assembly position, the section dug emplacements for the two guns with sandbag protection, observation posts, etc , the gunners assisting. The work was finished at dawn and the section moved back about 800 yards to guard the bullocks. About half an hour later the guns moved forward about 2,0C0 yards the sappers going ahead to prepare the road. The guns came into action in the open, the section again acting as guard to the bullocks.

In the meantime, the Flying Column and Column B had got into motion about 8.30 a.m. Of the former, the 76th advanced towards the Turkish second line, the cavalry dismounted attacking on the right. After advancing about a mile under heavy fire they were definitely checked about 10 a.m. and dug themselves in.

Column B (Brigadier General Hamilton; 18th Brigade) advanced about the same time with the Norfolks (right) and 110th in the front line and the 7th and 120th in support. At first the advance was unopposed but at 9.15 a.m. it came under fire from rifle pits in low scrub 500 yards in front. The enemy here were soon driven out and the front line continued to advance but was soon brought to a standstill by heavy rifle and machine gun fire from the main reserve of the 45th Turkish division, 900 yards distant.

During this advance the right half of 22nd Company with Matthews and Crawford stayed at Column B's rendezvous on the canal, guarding the reserve ammunition and medical units, and taking occasional shots at distant Arabs. At about noon they got orders to advance behind the 18th Brigade, which was done in open order, several casualties being incurred from rifle fire. The 18th Brigade had now pushed forward and captured some trenches in the reserve portion of the enemy's first line, but could make no further progress. The sappers lay out in the open behind the brigade. At about 3 p.m. Matthews, while bending over a wounded man to bandage his wrist, was hit in the backside by a spent bullet. Thinking that someone had kicked him, he turned round to abuse him but found himself addressing the desert. This blow gave him water on the knee, which was a nuisance in the retreat. This afternoon was very troublesome to the sappers as they were all the time under fire, but could see nothing to fire at and not being in the front line, could not relieve their feelings by firing into the blue.

About 9 a.m. Delamain attacked Vital Point with Column A, the 30th Brigade leading and the Dorsets, 104th and right half of the 22nd Company in reserve. The 30th Brigade had to advance some 5,000 yards and this was accomplished in rushes without firing, the artillery and machine guns giving effective covering fire. The Indian Infantry were checked momentarily by the wire but made their way through and drove the enemy out of the Vital Point about 10 a. m.—an amazing feet of arms. Portions of the units on the left, finding themselves under heavy fire from the work on their left, now swung round and pushed south along the trenches but could make little progress and Delamin pushed up half the Dorsets and the 104th to reinforce the right of the 30th Brigade still keeping in hand half the Dorsets and the right half of 22nd Company, which had so far not been heavily engaged. The remainder of the 30th Brigade thus reinforced pushed on, the units well mixed up and were finally held up about 800 yards short of the Turkish second line by the Turkish general reserve counter attacking about 1 p.m. About 2 p.m., the 30th Brigade began to give way before the Turkish counter attacks and retire on Vital Point. During the afternoon, Delamain himself collected such men as he could and tried to advance again but could do little more than hold off the enemy.

At about 5 p.m., Hamilton made a last attempt to advance; and for this, Matthews and his half company were pushed forward. They reached a trench which was occupied by the Norfolks, the sappers feeling it odd to be with them instead of their old friends the Dorsets, but before the attack developed, orders were received to break off the fight and fall back on Vital Point whither the 30th Brigade were already retiring. During this retreat, 22nd Company formed the rear guard. It was a difficult job trying to get the wounded of all regiments along in the dark, but it was believed that no one was left out in the desert alive. Jemadar Shankaram Pille did particularly good work on this occasion getting stragglers of all units along.

We must now turn to events on the left flank. As already stated, the 17th Brigade by 10.30 a.m., had got to within 700 yards of the enemy's trenches to the north-east of the High Wall. At about 11 a.m., General Hoghton received orders from the division to bring up his left shoulder and move on Vital Point. As a result he retired a short distance and moved across the enemy's front to his right and then turned in on the Water Redoubt. The two sections of 17th Company were still behind the 22nd Punjabis, but at about noon were ordered up to the same line. At this point, Gen. Hoghton sent for Loring and pointed out the Water Redoubt about 700 yards distant; which he said was holding up the attack and must be taken at all costs. He pointed out about hundred men of the Oxfords and 150 of the 22nd Punjabis, who were without British officers and had lost their way. He ordered Loring to take the redoubt with these men and his own half company. Loring organized his troops—Oxfords on the right, Sappers in the centre and 22nd on the left, and advanced. In spite of heavy fire the troops pushed forward, the enemy surrendering as our men reached the wire. Loring was shot through the lungs, the command devolving on Dunhill.

In the meantime, Gen. Townshend and his staff had arrived at Vital Point. Delamain had gone on with most of his troops in his abortive attack on the enemy's second line but had left behind half the Dorsets and the left half of the 22nd Company under Campbell. The D.E.C. had begged Delamain not to put the sappers into the original attack. Gen. Townshend now sent these troops under the command of Major Utterson, Dorsets, down the line to the left to assist the 17th Brigade's attack; and after severe fighting they succeeded in clearing the complicated trench line between Vital Point and the Water Redoubt about the same time as the 17th Brigade took the latter. During this fighting, Campbell was hit three times in the right shoulder and Garrett was killed by a bayonet wound, while leading his men down a trench.

Garrett had been with the company since Basra days. He had been a member of Messrs Siemens in Madras. He was a charming fellow and a good officer.

Having captured the Water Redoubt, parts of the 17th Brigade, with the two sections of 17th Company pushed down the trenches to the left and captured another redoubt (about due east of the arch) and about 400 yards from it. The enemy could now be seen retreating in large numbers from his right, but our troops only had about twenty rounds apiece left and pursuit was impossible.

This ended the fighting on the 22nd November. The 6th Division, with a rifle strength of 10,212, had driven the enemy, who, exclusive of the troops on the right bank, had 14,000 infantry, from the whole of their first line, capturing 1,650 prisoners. Our casualties had been 4,511, nearly all in the infantry and including 47 per cent of the officers.

The night found the men of all units and brigades in the greatest confusion. Matthews and his left half of the 22nd Company, covering the retirement of the 18th Brigade, reached Vital Point about midnight, very tired, hungry and thirsty. Boyes and No. 3 Section of 17th Company had moved about 3 p.m., with the five inch guns, to a position outside the wire at Vital Point, (making a road for them across some very deep nullahs on the way). During the night he got orders from the D.E.C. to leave his guns and collect all sappers of either company that he could find. But he could only find a few. Dunhill and his half of the 17th Company passed the night on the work that they had helped to capture to the south of the Water Redoubt.

The enemy had withdrawn completely to his second line during the night.

The trenches were full of enemy dead and wounded and our wounded were being brought in all night. The medical transport arrangements were inadequate to deal with the unexpectedly heavy casualties and every form of transport, principally A.T. carts, was requisitioned. In spite of the heroic efforts of the medical personnel the sufferings of the wounded were ghastly.

Next morning (23rd) was spent in reorganization.

The confusion after the fighting on the 22nd was very marked. The infantry had lost nearly all their British officers, and the men were wandering about in twos and threes looking for their units. It was not till mid-day on the 23rd that the force began to take shape again. The troops were mostly three or four miles from the river and everyone suffered severely from thirst. A heavy dust storm was blowing all day.

The 17th Brigade reorganised at Vital Point, which the enemy shelled spasmodically, and here Dunhill's half of 17th Company rejoined them. No. 3 Section (Boyes), with the few details they had collected, was ordered at 6.30 a.m. to rejoin their five inch guns and stayed with them during the day at a point south-east of Vital Point. At one period they were threatened by Arab cavalry but some infantry came up and the Sappers did not have to fire. About 3 p.m., it was decided to move the guns 500 yards to the south, and later behind the wire at Vital Point. During these moves the Sappers had to prepare the road and also cover the guns on the outer flank, where they kept off the Arab cavalry. During the night, the section took up a position at the south-east corner of Vital Point. The 17th Company throughout this day were still without food and water.

The right half of the 22nd Company remained at Vital Point, where the 18th Brigade were reorganizing. Here most of the survivors of the left half company, left without any British officers, found them. Divisional headquarters had moved to High Wall in the morning, and orders were received in the afternoon for the 18th Brigade to move there. The 22nd Company went with them, and here the rest of left half company found them. Here also, after dark, they got food and water.

The cavalry, 2/7th Gurkha Rifles and 24th Punjabis, had, in the meanwhile, taken up a position near Ctesiphon Arch, the infantry on a mound, afterwards known as Gurkha Mound.

During the afternoon of the 23rd the whole of the Turks

moved out of their second line. On their right, the 35th and 38th Divisions were held off at first by artillery fire, and later by hard infantry fighting from Gurkha Mound. On their left, the 45th and 51st Divisions, after 4 p.m., advanced against our front from the Water Redoubt to Vital Point, the bulk of the 51st Division moving round to envelop the latter. At dusk the attack developed along the front but luckily the 51st Division lost its way and its attack never developed. The attack mostly fell on Water Redoubt and Gurkha Mound and was everywhere repulsed; the garrison of Gurkha Mound behaving with especial gallantry.

The 22nd Company at High Wall were not involved in the night fighting. Dunhill's half of 17th Company was, at dusk, on the east face of Vital Point, shortly afterwards they were withdrawn and placed in reserve behind the mound. During the night they dug emplacements for two guns on the east face and several shelters for reserves, headquarters, etc., on the mound, enclosed by the work. They also assisted with rifle fire in repelling one of the attacks.

No. 3 Section, 17th Company, took up a position on the right of the 76th Punjabis, on the south-east point of Vital Point, but were not attacked directly; at 3.30 a.m. on the 24th, the five inch guns were moved to High Wall, the section making the road for them through very difficult country.

By dawn, the enemy, in a state of great despondency, had every where withdrawn to their second line.

During the 24th, the whole of the British force concentrated at High Wall. Gen. Hoghton and the 17th Brigade evacuated Vital Point about 5 p.m. having sent back all their wounded. Dunhill with his half of 17th Company and the Oxfords covered the 17th Brigade's retirement. They were heavily sniped on the way but reached High Wall at 6.30 p.m. where they were joined by Boyes and No. 3 Section and the whole company (barring No. 4 Section) bivouacked together. The men at last got some food and water.

A certain amount of work was done at High Wall putting the position into a state of defence. Machine gun emplacements were dug along the mounds, some new trenches dug and Turkish trenches that were not needed, filled in.

At High Wall, Lieut. H. S. Cheshire, I.A.R.O. joined the 22nd Company, which was very short of officers. He had been acting as field engineer with the cavalry brigade and was in peace a fairly senior P.W.D. officer. He remained with the company till the end of the siege of Kut.

The night of the 24th/25th passed quietly. In the early morning, a large number of Arabs rode up to the bivouac, under the impression that it was a Turkish force. One of their leaders rode up to General Townshend and was actually seized before he found out his mistake. Both sides were equally puzzled. There was a good deal of indiscriminate firing some officers directed their men to fire and some shouting "Dont fire". The Sappers did not fire. The Arabs eventually got away with little loss.

During the night 24th/25th, the Turks, on hearing that the British were again advancing, lost their nerve and began to retreat in some confusion behind the Diyala. They might have gone as far as Baghdad, but on the way they met their 5th Division, part of Khalil Bey's 18th Corps, which had made a wonderful march from Mosul, on its way to reinforce the Tigris front. This stopped the rout and the whole army re-occupied their second line.

During the afternoon, General Townshend decided to retire to Lajj and at 5 p.m. issued orders accordingly.

Just before the 22nd Company moved back, they were told to demolish a Turkish gun. This turned out to be a magnificent old bronze mortar, of 15 inch calibre and covered with Turkish text. It seemed very harmless and too interesting to destroy, so it was left. This is believed to be the mortar known to the garrison of Kut as Flatulent Flossie. It fired bronze spherical shells about 1 inch thick. Fragments of it when polished up made very nice ash trays. No one was known to have been hurt by one of these shells, but there was great competition to get the fragments and one man was nearly wounded through standing too close to a shell waiting for it to explode.

The casulties amongst Indian other ranks of the two companies at the battle of Ctesiphon were:—

17th Company 2 killed and 12 wounded.

22nd Company 8 killed; the number of wounded in this company is not known but it must have been about thirty.

CHAPTER XI.

The Retreat to Kut-Al-Amara.

The march commenced at 7.30 p.m. and the force reached Lajj at 2.30 a.m. on the 26th. The three sections of the 17th Company acted as escort to the five inch guns. They widened the road at the end of the Wall (north face of camp) before starting. The road was very bad and they were unable to improve it as it was at least two feet thick in dust. It was very dark when the march began and it was difficult to keep to the road. One of the five inch guns went off the road into a large hole, but the Sappers dug a ramp for the wheels, and with all the gunners and sappers on the drag ropes, and the bullocks pulling, the gun was got out. Soon afterwards the moon rose, the road got better, and the march was ended without further mishap. The 22nd Company was with the main body, available for road work but not actually employed.

On arrival, all turned in and slept well in spite of the cold and a slight drizzle. In the morning, tents were got out from the ships and erected; the two companies being together.

The Army Commander wanted the 6th Division to hold Lajj; so a position for the whole division was traced. This gave plenty of work for the sappers and the troops actually began digging the position, the sappers doing some wiring.

East and No. 1 Section of 17th Company had been attached to the Bridging Train since 21st November, when the advance from Lajj began, and remained with them till they arrived at Kut. On the 22nd the bridge was dismantled at 1 p.m. presumably in expectation of an advance, but was ordered to be reconstructed, which was completed by 8 p.m.

On the 23rd it was again dismantled.

On the 25th at 8 p.m. urgent orders were received to reconstruct the bridge, which was done, with the help of acetylene flares, by 4 a.m. on the 26th. East and his section actually rejoined 17th Company on the 27th.

At 2 p.m. on the 27th orders for a further retirement were received and East and his section went back to the Bridging Train. Orders had been received by the latter to get away by 4 p.m., this was done by forming rafts and cutting the anchor cables. The river was full of boats bolting. One tow got ashore and stuck. The launch with Sandes and East also ran ashore and was got off with difficulty. Aziziyah was reached at 10 a.m. on 28th. Bridge was commenced at once and completed by 7 p.m., the stranded tow luckily turning up.

The rest of the two Sapper companies marched with the remainder of the force at 4 p.m. to Aziziyah arriving at 5 a.m. on the 28th. Tents were left standing to the last moment to deceive the enemy, and those and all possible stores were burnt by the navy before they left.

At Aziziyah, the division halted two days to evacuate the wounded and as many stores as possible ; on the 29th, parties were sent to sort out the companies' kit which had been left at the Serai before the advance. It was hoped to get this away on the boats but ultimately it was abandoned. During the time at Aziziyah, the bivouac was visited by a very heavy dust storm. One officer unrolled his bedding and took his eyes off it and in a few minutes it was so nearly buried in dust that he had great difficulty in finding it ; a lot of kit was lost this way.

Here the British force was reinforced by the 14th Huzzars and two companies of ths 2nd Royal West Kents. The former got going at once. One of our ships, the Shaitan, had sunk some miles up stream and salvage was being impeded by Arab snipers. The Cavalry Brigade went out on the 29th to help and the Huzzars caught a hundred Arabs in a bend of the river and annihilated them.

During this stay at Aziziyah, no engineer work of any importance was done ; the force largely employed itself in making up the deficit in rations from the last week. Apparently Gen. Townshend never intended to make a stand here, though Gen. Nixon wished to. Some work, however, was done on the old defences, and on piers for barges.

The wounded from Ctesiphon had, in the meantime, been sent downstream. Matthews saw Campbell on the morning of the 23rd on a cart, one of a convoy going to the river. Loring was left for dead, outside the Water Redoubt, where he had been hit. His experiences are best recorded in his own words :

" My first recollections after recovering consciousness on the battlefield were those of uncertainty as to where I was, as it was too cold for hell and not warm enough for heaven. I was eventually picked up by a wandering stretcher party of the Combined Field Ambulance and taken to the dressing station, which was in a Turkish trench, at the bottom of which the wounded were placed. We were kept there all that night and the next day and evacuated back to the river in the early hours of the second night—nothing to eat and very little to drink. The humorous side to waiting was during a lull in the day, I heard the voice of Dunhill and Baryam Singh asking if my body was there, as the company wanted to bury me! During the Turkish counterattack, the enemy got within 100 yards of the trench where the wounded were lying. The second night, somewhere about 1 a.m., an order came through to evacuate the wounded to the river, those who could walk had to walk the rest went in A.T. carts and one motor ambulance, holding four lying down cases. I was one of those selected by the R.A.M.C. colonel to go in the motor, it was a not unmixed blessing as the springs were designed for Piccaddilly and not for a cross country journey in Mespotamia. The river bank was reached at about 3.30 a.m., and we were put on steamers and barges and sent off to Kut, which was reached without incident. There were, of course, no bunks or beds and we were first placed on the decks. At Kut we were put on another ship—still no beds, but we managed to raise a certain number of blankets out of Kut. We made two unsuccessful attempts to get out of Kut but were unable to do so owing to the Arabs lining the banks and shooting at the ship. There was no protection on the ships and barges against the bullets and a number of wounded were killed or wounded again. Eventually a third attempt was made, as Gen. Nixon now wished to get back to Basra, aud this time we were helped by H.M.S. Butterfly, a mountain battery and half battalion 67th Punjabis. We got through with little difficulty and reached Amara, where we dropped those wounded who required early operations, and so on to Basra without further incident. We had one medical officer for 600 wounded and were lucky if we got our dressings changed every third or fourth day. It took us 16 days to get from Ctesiphon to Basra, and, until we got to Amara, we lived mostly on stew and cold water. Those of us who were transferred to the Varela on arrival at Basra, revelled in a decent bunk and the first respectable meal for several months. The report of the commission on Mespotamia describes the condition of the particular ship and accompanying barges that I travelled on ".

Loring eventually reached India in December. He made

an amazingly quick recovery from the bullet wound through his lungs. He was given three months sick leave, most of which he spent in an office at Kirkee, working at his mens accounts and intimidating his friends by violent fits of coughing.

Campbell was evacuated to England. He never recovered the use of his arm though this did not prevent him taking part in two more campaigns of the Great War and hunting up to the year of his death in 1930.

The Turks were reported to be at El Kutunieh on the 29th. General Townshend therefore decided to withdraw from Aziziyah on the 30th. At 2 p.m. on 29th, the Bridging Train got orders to be ready to move by 4 p.m. They formed their bridge into rafts, cut their anchor cables and got off in time. East and his Section of 17th Company were still with them. The adventures of the Bridging Train till it reached Kut form a very interesting chapter of "In Kut and Captivity". It is enough here to say that miraculously enough it did arrive though with very little bridging gear.

Gen. Melliss, with the 16th Cavalry, 30th Infantry Brigade and No. 3 Section of 17th Company under Boyes, left Aziziyah at 8 a.m. and marched 20 miles down stream. The road was good and needed no work. The remainder of the force spent the morning in destroying all warlike stores, taking up barbed wire and throwing it into the river and left Aziziyah at 11 a.m. and marched to Um-At-Tabul, 10 miles. Here they went into a perimeter camp on the river bank.

The same day (30th November) the Turks reached Aziziyah and halted. Just before sunset they resumed their march and their advanced guard gained touch with and exchanged shots with our outposts about 8 p.m. The Turks thinking they had driven back our rearguard went into camp and orders were issued to continue the pursuit at 9 a.m. next day.

Gen. Townshend grasped the situation but was unable to retreat at once owing to the presence of his shipping which could not move at night. He issued orders for the shipping and land transport to move as soon as it was light and sent orders to Gen. Melliss to move back to his assistance.

Before dawn on December 1st the division prepared to deploy; the 16th Brigade was to hold the north-west face of the camp, the 18th and 17th Brigades to prolong the line and the cavalry to be on the extreme right. The Sappers were with the batteries for escort and road making, the 22nd

Company being with the 82nd Field Battery. (It is noteworthy that the old practice in Indian manoeuvres of using the sappers as escort to guns was very common in this campaign and contributed greatly to the mobility of the guns).

Dawn exhibited the Turkish camp 2,000 yards away and their troops commencing to deploy. The fight started with the 82nd Battery opening fire. The cavalry and their horse guns went off into the desert at full gallop, and as the brigades deployed, all the guns opened battery fire and the cavalry began to envelop the Turkish left.

Two regiments of the 51st Turkish division which had commenced to advance, were checked. The remaining three divisions simply bolted. There seemed to be an opportunity for a surprising victory but Gen. Townshend who had meant to attack simply to disengage and who suspected the presence of Turkish reinforcements, countermanded the attack and ordered a withdrawal which was begun immediately and conducted with great precision under heavy artillery fire. During this part of the action Dunhill was killed. The exact circumstances are unknown. As no British officer was left with the 17th Company, the D.E.C. placed Lieut. Spink, I.A.R.O. in charge. The Sappers now acted as infantry, taking their turn in the rearguard as the division leapfrogged back. Towards noon, Matthews found some Sappers carrying Dunhill along on a stretcher. He was quite dead so he buried him near the road.

The Turks, such as remained on the field, started to pursue, but the infantry did not come far. The cavalry and guns continued the pursuit till 11 a.m.

Meanwhile Gen. Melliss' force had started to march back about 6.30 a.m. and after about six miles met the division retreating and came into line between the 17th Brigade and the cavalry. Boyes' section was attached to the Hants howitzer battery of Gen. Melliss' force which came into action against the enemy's extreme left. They had very hard work filling in nullahs and making roads for the guns to retire. At 11 a.m. this section met the rest of 17th Company (2 and 4 Sections) under Spink and Boyes took charge of the whole. The retreat continued throughout the day and at 10 p.m. the force arrived at Qala Shadi (Monkey Village) and bivouacked. This was a 26 miles march (30 for Melliss' force) in addition to the action. A good many men, especially followers were lost in the night part of the march. The night was bitterly cold and the 17th Company transport could not be located; but Boyes managed to borrow a few blankets and a little atta.

This long march shook off the pursuit and no more Turkish regulars were seen till some days after the troops arrived in Kut. Arabs however harassed the force considerably.

The most serious losses at Ummat Tabul occured among the shipping. Our ships came immediately under fire and the gunboats had to stay to guard the retreat of the rest. Two were lost and the general retreat of the river craft was most precarious (See "In Kut and Captivity").

Early next morning, the 17th Company handed over all their guncotton to 22nd Company. There was a bridge over the nullah south-west of the village and as soon as all the troops were clear, Matthews blew it up. This bridge was of grey stone, presumably from the Pusht-i-Kuh. The march commenced at 6 a.m. and continued till midday when a three hour halt was made on the river bank and the remains of whatever food any one had was eaten. In most cases no one had any at all. There was a certain amount of sniping from the right bank of the river by Arabs, but not enough to worry the troops much.

At 3 p.m. the march was resumed and continued along a good road till 9 p.m. to a point four miles from Kut. Rations already cooked were sent out from the town to meet the troops; unfortunately very few units discovered them. But both companies were lucky enough to do so and got a generous and much appreciated supply. It was a bitterly cold night and no one got much sleep though all were tired out.

The march from Umm-At-Tubul to this halt had been 44 miles (51 for Gen. Melliss' column). After the pursuit had been shaken off, the brigades marched, independently At Qala Shadi the leading brigade had marched off from its bivouac before the rear brigade got in; so the hours given are approximate only. The general impression of the troops was that the march was continuous with short halts the whole way. The official history speaks of many men dropping out from exhaustion during the march and being picked up by carts. Only one sapper got such a ride. The remainder, through very tired, completed the march.

On the 3rd, the force was marched into Kut arriving at 9 a.m. The two Sapper companies went into bivouac in the most northerly palm grove on the river bank above the town. Here East and No. 1 Section of 17th Company rejoined having arrived after their adventurous trip with the Bridging Train the previous afternoon. The march was very slow; everyone was tired and footsore but the road was easy.

The Retreat was over.

Seven N.C.O.s and men of the 17th Company were wounded in the engagement at Umm-at-Tabul.

CHAPTER XII.

Siege of Kut-Al-Amara
First phase. Defence against the Turks.

Kut-Al-Amara lies in the south-east corner of a U shaped bend in the Tigris, 1½ miles across at the base, and two miles deep. Since its capture at the end of September, it had been prepared as an advanced base under the orders of Maj. General Rimington, the Engineer-in-Chief of the force. At the north east corner of the bend, on the river bank, quarters for an Indian battalion, a general hospital and engineer, ordnance and supply parks were enclosed in a high wall of 1,400 yards perimeter, forming a defensible post called the Fort. From this there extended across the neck of the peninsula a double apron fence laid out in long Vs, behind the reentrants of which were four blockhouses, numbered 1,2,3,4, from the right. Some 300 yards in front of the wire were a line of sandhills. The intention of these works was, of course, defence against raids, not against an organized siege.

A river convoy, consisting largely of engineer stores, came up just before the arrival of the 6th Division.

There was an old Turkish bridge across the Tigris about one mile below the Fort.

The transport of the 6th Division arrived in Kut on 2nd December, and the troops, very weary, on the 3rd. The 17th Company was met by East and No. 1 Section, who had arrived the day before with the Bridging Train and who showed them their bivouac site in a walled enclosure in the palmgroves, eight hundred yards north-east of the town. The 22nd Company bivouacked alongside them and the 48th Pioneers near by. The other engineer units in Kut were the Sirmur I.S. Sappers and Miners under Captain C. E. Colbeck, R.E. in the Fort and the Bridging Train, who, after the first few days, were employed in the town.

The rest of the 3rd and 4th December were spent in resting and in digging "funk-pits" and what were called dug outs for officers. These were lightly roofed with corrugated sheet iron, covered with about six inches of earth. They were, of course, only splinter proof and many of the Kut dugouts were only roofed with canvas. No one expected them to be occupied for long and in any case deep dugouts would have been uninhabitable during the flood period. The 17th Company mess dugout, which shortly became a combined mess dugout, was 12 feet by 9 feet and 7 feet deep.

On the 4th, the 17th Company also erected an observation tower on the roof of the headquarters building in Kut. As soon as it was erected, it was ordered to be dismantled, a little later to be erected again and later still again to be dismantled. Platforms for observation were also erected inside the brickkilns, north-west of Kut, and these were left standing.

The officers of the two companies, on arrival in Kut were :—

17th Company.	22nd Company.
Lieut. A. T. East, I.A.R.O.,	Lt. A. B. Matthews, M.C. R.E.,
,, W. R. Boyes, I.A.R.O,	,, K. B. S. Crawford, R.F.,
	,, H. S. Cheshire, I.A.R.O.

Lieut. W. Spink, I.A.R.O., (attached temporarily)

Sub. Baryam Singh, I.O.M.,	Sub. Mohammad Din, I.O.M.,
Jem. Fateh Khan, I.D.S.M.,	Jem. Shankaram Pille.
,, Krishna Bhonsle.	

On arrival, Lieut. Spink reverted to assistant field engineer. Crawford was transferred to 17th Company to take command. Lieut. W.H. Mathias, 128th Pioneers, attached to S. & T.C., asked to be employed with Sappers and Miners and, though senior to Matthews, volunteered to serve under him and was posted to 22nd Company.

Most of the artificers of the two companies and of the 48th Pioneers were taken away from the companies at once and formed into R. E. workshops (near the D. E. C's. quarters in Kut) under C.S.M. Bellis, Sgts. Toleman, and Baker. These were kept busy throughout the siege with manufactures of all kinds, including hand and rifle grenades, periscopes, trench mortars, periscope rifles for snipers, pickets for entanglements, trench ladders and bridges, cookers for crude oil, etc. The grenades played an important part in the repulse of the great Turkish attack on Christmas Eve.

Material was always a difficulty and endless improvisation was necessary and great ingenuity shown. The official history says:—

"The sappers in Kut did excellent work during December, in improvising siege weapons of warfare, with which the division had not been equipped. At first the Turks had a great advantage over the garrison in the matter of bombs, but the sappers soon put matters on a better footing. Commandeering every available mirror in the place they turned out a sufficient supply of periscopes and they devised a few efficient and ingenious trench mortars, at first from wood and then from the cylinders of a 70 H.P. Gnome engine".

Captain Stace, R.E., was in charge of these workshops.

As soon as Gen. Townshend decided to stand at Kut, a new defensive position was laid out and the infantry commenced to dig and wire this on the 4th. There is no doubt, judging by subsequent events, that the sandhills should have been held as our front line. At the cost of adding 800 yards to the front line it would have kept the Turks a mile further from Kut and denied them observation and it would have saved endless trouble during the floods; but the time factor led to a decision to hold the line of the existing obstacle. The front line consisted of the Fort and four redoubts A, B, C & D, each for a company, at the forward reentrants of the wire, and connected by a line of fire trenches.

A second line, selected by the G.S.O. I of the division, was laid out by the D.E.C. It ran from about one mile behind the Fort on the east to half a mile behind the front line on the west. It had one bad salient to include some old trenches.

A keep was also laid out round Kut town, the line including the brick kilns redoubt and some walled enclosures.

Works to be held by two battalions were also laid out round Woolpress village, on the right bank, opposite Kut. There were also picquet posts all along the left bank of the river inside the defences. The defences were divided into the following sections:—

(1). North-east section. Three picquets south of the Fort, the Fort and the front line to B Redoubt exclusive (inclusive after 21st January). This section was held permanently by the 17th Brigade (Brigadier General Hoghton).

(2). North-west section—remainder of the front line. This was held alternately by the 16th Brigade (Maj. General Delamain) and the 30th Brigade (Maj. General Melliss, V.C.), the brigade, not in line, forming the general reserve.

(3). The town of Kut, Woolpress village and the remaining river piquets were held permanantly by the 18th Brigade (Brigadier General Hamilton).

(4). The second line of defence was held by the general reserve. This brigade, however, soon started some support trenches 300-400 yards behind the front line. These were later connected up and extended to the river on either side. This system was called the middle line and became the location of the general reserve. It was completed about 25th December.

At the beginning of the siege, the engineer work in the north east section normally fell to the Sirmur Sappers, who were quartered in the Fort. The 22nd Company were employed in the north west section and the 17th Company were employed all over the area as decided by the D.E.C.

The two brigades, alternately holding the north-west section and commanded by two generals of strong personality, rarely agreed, and were apt to use the sappers as a channel for mutual recrimination. The 22nd Company avoided taking part in these rows, but there is no doubt where their sympathies lay. They had been with the 16th Brigade in every fight except Ctesiphon, and General Delamain, on receiving his promotion for brilliant service, had included the company in his order thanking the units of his brigade for gaining him the honour. There had been close friendship between the Dorsets and the company ever since the race for the trenches at Sahil; and when the sappers worked in the vicinity of the Dorsets, the work could be entrusted to a junior non-commissioned officer with the certainity that the infantry would help and co-operate. This could not not be said of other infantry battalions, where the presence of a R.E. officer, with the working parties, was necessary. A similar friendship existed between the 22nd Company and the 82nd Battery, R.F.A., whose battery position was near their bivouac. A gunner of this battery was always welcome in the 22nd Company lines.

During the 4th, all the shipping except H.M.S. Samana, a few motor boats, 6 barges and forty or fifty mahelas, went down stream. The same day the Sirmur Sappers dismantled the old

Turkish bridge and collected the timber on the bank near the Fort. On the 5th, it was decided that the 6th Cavalry Brigade was to proceed down stream and the Bridging Train commenced reconstructing a bridge near the Fort. This was completed on the 6th, and after some delay while a gap at the far end, which had been believed fordable, was bridged, the brigade with all its transport and hordes of camels crossed. S Battery, R.H.A., left two of its fifteen pounders behind. The Bridging Train then started dismantling, but were delayed while some snipers were being dislodged and did not finish till 3 a.m. next morning.

The Turks appeared about 4 p.m., on the 5th, and were engaged by our covering troops on the sandhills, and at 5 p.m. they opened artillery fire on the Fort and the hospital tents, which were very conspicuous in the open near the palm groves, (the hospitals were moved into Kut next day.) The bombardment was repeated on the 6th and 7th.

The infantry had been busy digging. By the evening of the 6th, the fire trenches of the front and second lines were down to a depth of two feet six inches.

During the first days of the siege the Sapper Companies were naturally very busy. Matthews under Gen. Delamain's order laid out the front line on the 4th and Boyes assisted the D.E.C. in laying out the second line. Two sections of 22nd Company under Crawford went over to Woolpress on the 3rd and spent three days on the defences of the village. On the 5th, Boyes and one section of 17th Company drew timber and wiring material from the Fort. On the 6th, both companies were wiring in front of the second line. On the 7th, both companies, during the morning, completed the wiring of the second line and commenced trebling the double apron fence of the front line and wiring round the redoubts. The Turks were shelling the Fort and two sappers were killed and one wounded while drawing material. East also put a few land mines down in front of the first line.

On the 6th, the officers of the two companies decided to mess together in the 17th Company's dugout. In the afternoon of the 7th, Crawford and Boyes went into the town to purchase mess stores. The siege was expected to last two months, but three months' stores were purchased to cover all contingencies.

While the wiring was going on on the 7th, Matthews, Mathias (who had joined on the 6th) and C.S.M. Bellis, blew up the four blockhouses. These were square, mudbrick, two storied buildings, about twenty feet square, containing a lot of timber. They were demolished by four charges each of six pounds of guncotton, buried in the fire step on the ground floor at each corner. The mounds of debris were later converted into snipers' posts and the timber and corrugated sheet iron came in very useful in roofing dugouts in the front line.

During these first days, the 17th Company also put up protection for lift and force pumps on the river bank. The river was at this period nearly thirty feet below the top of the bank and the pumping stations had to be installed some way down.

Hardly had the Bridging Train finished dismantling the bridge at the Fort in the early hours of the 7th, when they got orders to construct another considerably nearer Kut town. A covering party was landed on the far bank by the Samana. One section of the 17th Company assisted the Bridging Train, but the latter were naturally tired out, and material had to be fetched from a distance; so the bridge was not completed that night when the covering party was withdrawn.

In the afternoon, Turkish Infantry appeared advancing from the north-east and, in spite of our shell fire, established themselves in a nala, 450 yards from the Fort, and by next morning they had dug themselves in for a length of 900 yards.

On the night of the 7th/8th, both companies wired in the front line and completed the second apron of the fence. Three men were wounded. About 11 p.m., a motor car suddenly ran up to the front line bringing Captain Stace, R.E., and some other officers, who were going to lay observation mines. They had meant to leave the car at the second line and had run through it by mistake. This drew quite a lot of fire and stopped the work for some time.

On the 8th the Bridging Train and No. 1 Section of 17th Company continued the bridge and in spite of shelling, completed it. At this point Sandes discovered that he had no covering party. On his reporting this, 200 men of the 67th Punjabis, under Captain Gribbon, went across and took up a covering position.

During this day, one section of 22nd Company under Mathias repaired wire in the front line, until our cavalry patrols, which had been holding the sandhills, were finally driven in about 11 a.m. After this no work above ground could be done in the front line by day. After dark, the remainder of 17th Company and half the 22nd Company, under Matthews, finished the wiring of the front line, while the other half of 22nd Company under Mathias went across the bridge to wire the bridge head. The position here was a weak one, as the ground in front was very broken, but it was the only possible position. Mathias had difficulty in bringing up material as his transport did not turn up, but he got a single apron fence round the line thickening it in the nalas.

On the 9th the Turks bombarded Kut town and the Fort in the morning, and one 16 pounder shell came through the roof of the dugout when Matthews, Mathias and Cheshire were sleeping off their nights' work. By some miracle no one was killed though Mathias was hit in the shoulder by a small fragment. He had to go to hospital that afternoon.

At 8 a.m., the Turks attacked the bridge head and drove the detachment of the 67th across the bridge. General Melliss, however, ordered them to retake it which they did with the bayonet; but Gribbon was killed and his subaltern badly wounded. General Melliss, who had followed across the bridge, finding the position hopeless, withdrew the survivors. Sandes who was on the near bank rallied the men as they arrived and remained there till the 2/7th Gurkha Rifles came up and took up a position to cover the bridge.

After the loss of the bridgehead, it was decided to destroy the bridge. Lieut. Sweet 2/7th Gurkha Rifles volunteered to destroy it at night by cutting the anchor ropes, but Sandes was doubtful as to the result. At 1 p.m., the D.E.C. sent for the sapper officers and asked for volunteers for the operation, explaining the hazardous nature of the work. Matthews volunteered and was given the task. He selected volunteers from his company to help him. These included Naik Sohan Singh, Spr. Indar Singh, and Spr. Abdul Aziz. Matthews' original plan was to take two charges of guncotton slabs, fixed between boards 13 feet long (corresponding to the width of the bridge). One charge was to have a long fuze which was to be lit before starting and carried as far as possible along the bridge; the intention being that if the carrying party were knocked out, the bridge would anyhow be cut somewhere. The enemy of course were not merely covering the bridge but able to fire straight along it at close range and it seemed certain that they would have machine guns sweeping it. The other charge was to be laid on the shore bay and let off as soon as the first party had got back.

Matthews practised his men during the afternoon and went to the bridge at dark. Here he was told that the fourth and fifth boats (local danaks) had sunk and that the planking of the sunk bay had been ripped off by the current. The Turks on the far bank, however, seemed quiet.

At this point, Lieut. Sweet came up and told Matthews that there were still some wounded on the far bank and that he wished to go across and bring them in; he believed that the Turks were not actually occupying the bridge head. Matthews pointed out that, even if this supposition were true, this enterprise would be very difficult, and that if the bridge head were occupied, any such attempt would make the destruction of the bridge impossible. After a good deal of discussion, Sweet gave up his plan but said that he wished to help Matthews with the bridge, and that, if there was no interference, he would go across afterwards in a boat and look for the wounded men. Matthews accepted this offer and the party eventually consisted of the two officers, six sappers and six Gurkhas.

At 9 p.m. the party went forward. The Sappers carried the charge, straddling across the baulks of the sunken bay, Matthews with the port fire under his coat. Matthews then lit the fuze which was timed for ten minutes and he and one sapper carried the charge along the bridge. The remaining sappers and Gurkhas were dropped on the way, each being allotted to about six pontoons or boats and cutting half the anchor cables immediately; the Gurkhas being dropped first. Matthews and his sapper went forward till about four bays distant from the far end. Here they could hear the Turks talking but no fire was opened. They laid the charge and walked back. As they reached each ropeman, the remaining anchor ropes were cut in succession and the whole party reached the near bank just as the charge detonated.

The charge detonated successfully and cut the bridge; but the latter did not swing into the left bank as intended but broke into two pieces, a lot of the pontoons were lost and were seen next day stranded on sand banks down the river. The inshore charge was never lit.

After the explosion, Sweet endeavoured to carry out his rescue plan; but the Turks were now thoroughly alert. His boat attracted heavy fire at once and he had to give up his gallant attempt.

General Townshend recommended the two officers for the Victoria Cross and the men for the Indian Order of Merit; but the crosses were not awarded. He says in his account: "These two officers volunteered for what appeared to be certain death for the enemy had this bridge at the mercy of their rifles at 300—400 yards range and were firing down on it. They waited all day to carry out the operation under cover of darkness—a very different proceeding from doing it on the impulse of the moment".

At about 3 p.m., on the 10th, the Turks advanced all along our front line and though shelled heavily, dug themselves in about 450 yards from our trenches, and consolidated their position during the night.

Both field companies were out wiring during the night; the 17th Company putting up a double apron fence from a point in the front line wire, 100 yards from the river on the left, to a point 150 yards higher up on the river.

The Turkish artillery was pretty active. There was a heavy bombardment on the 10th and the north east bastion of the Fort was badly damaged. One sapper of the 17th Company was also killed in billets. This led to work by the 22nd Company in the Fort that night. Every night also the Turks used to let off thousands of rounds in the hope of catching our working parties. Casualties from this cause were pretty numerous during the first two months of the siege. The Turks had another trick of suddenly breaking out into heavy rifle fire at night, followed by cheering as if about to attack, but our men soon got used to this and took no notice except to send over a few starshells to make sure that no real attack was coming. Such fire was generally high and did no damage at any rate to the garrison. The Turks at night also suffered a good deal from "wind up".

On the night of the 12th/13th the Turks did, however, open a heavy attack on D Redoubt, which was repulsed by the 16th Brigade. The Sappers were only concerned in that their work was badly interfered with. The orders were that in an emergency of this kind, the Sappers and Pioneers came under the orders of the G.O.C., Reserve.

During the 11th both sides pushed on with their trenches. On the night of the 11th/12th, the Turks advanced and dug themselves in some 250 yards from our front line. From this time on they sapped forward making parallels and steadily approaching our trenches. They were wonderful diggers.

Our troops were digging also. On the 11th the fire trenches were three feet deep and communication trenches were started, though at first they were mere scratches in the ground. They were:—

    River Communication Trench from Fort to middle line and continuing as 24th Communication Trench to second line.

    Gurkha Communication Trench from A Redoubt to Second line.

    Reserve Communication Trench from B Redoubt to middle line only.

    67th Communication Trench from C Redoubt to second line.

    Hants Communication Trench from D Redoubt to second line.

From the second line to Kut, Brick Kiln Communication Trench and 30th Communication Trench were constructed, roughly in prolongation of 24th and Gurkha Communication Trenches and Hants Communication Trench was prolonged into the town.

The Sappers took plenty of part in these activities. On the night of the 11th, the 17th Company dug communication trenches in the Sapper lines, and the 22nd Company commenced the Brick Kiln Communication Trench; and on the night of the 13th/14th, the 17th Company and the 48th Pioneers commenced Hants Communication Trench. This communication trench between the front and the second line, was built straight with island traverses, very useful as passing places. The other communication trenches were of normal zig zag lay out.

Till these communication trenches were started, walking above ground by day and particularly between the Sapper lines and the town was very dangerous owing to snipers. The communication trenches were three feet deep by the 14th, and by the 21st they were deep enough to walk about without stooping—a great relief.

It was believed that the old hospital huts were being used as ranging marks; so these were ordered to be destroyed. East and a party of 17th Company did this with explosives on the night of the 13th/14th and incidentally annexed a lot of useful timber and some good books which had been abandoned.

From the 14th December, the principal sapper work was mining. The Turkish saps were getting pretty close, and it was decided to construct defensive mines towards their sap-heads. Matthews was put in charge of this mining and the work was done by his company, assisted by parties of the 17th Company. Three mines were started on the 14th, No. 1 from D. Redoubt, No. 2 from the site of the demolished blockhouse No. 3, and No. 3 from north-west corner of C Redoubt. Mathias took up his quarters in D Redoubt to superintend the work, and remained there till it was finished. Mining parties worked four hours on and eight off; two senior N.C.Os. supervised each mine, relieving one another every 24 hours, and two I.Os., took charge of the whole work each for 24 hours.

No. 4 mine was started on the 15th, from the north-east corner of C Redoubt.

These mines were run about 13 feet below ground level, below which water interfered. No. 1 had a vertical shaft but all the others commenced with inclined galleries. The galleries were 2 feet 6 inches wide and 3 feet high with arched roofs. No frames or other support were required.

Progress was slow at first, largely owing to the fire trenches being crowded. The advance was from six to nine inches per hour. From the 17th. Infantry parties were used to haul earth away and endless ropes, to which bags of earth were attached, were rigged up in the mines. East, who had been a mining engineer in civil life, suggested using earth angurs to honey comb the face. These were made up in R.E. workshops and tried but without much success.

The Turks were also suspected of mining near the Fort. This led to a most successful trench raid on the night of the 19th/20th by parties of the 103rd and 119th accompanied by Colbeck and detachments of the Sirmur Sappers. No mines were found, but forty Turks were killed and eleven prisoners brought back; and some trenches also filled in.

Later on in the month, the Turks were suspected of mining in front of C Redoubt, where huge mounds of earth were appearing, but listening failed to detect any. Our men used to fire at the shovels of the Turkish Sappers, as they appeared above ground, to annoy them. Once after a shovel had been hit, it re-appeared a few minutes later with a first aid bandage fastened over the " wound ".

On the 18th, candles for the mines gave out and wicks floating in shallow tins of ghee were used. The checking of direction by this means was difficult and far from pleasant.

On the 21st, as No. 2, 3 and 4 mines were 90 feet out and under our wire, they were teed; No. 1 being still kept straight on. On the 22nd, two mines (5 and 6) were started branching out from one shaft in the listening post in front of C Redoubt. These two with No. 3 and 4 were to make a complete chain in front of this work.

The mines were very hot and stuffy. The men used to work in them stripped to the waist, leaving their clothes at the mine head. Outside it was very cold and while putting on their clothes men used to get chills which developed sometimes into pneumonia. Orders were issued that the men were to dress before leaving the mines but there were still cases of pneumonia.

After 2, 3 and 4 mines had been teed out 30 feet, all the mines were charged by the 22nd Company on the 31st December and 1st January. 5 and 6 and each branch of 2, 3 and 4 were loaded with two charges of 60 lbs. of guncotton and No. 1 with two charges of 70 lbs. In each mine the charges were placed in recesses above and below at opposite corners of the gallery. The idea was that the top charge was to be exploded first, followed by the lower if the Turks occupied the crater—a somewhat optimistic arrangement. Each charge had two electrically fired detonators and was tamped with sandbags and thirty feet of earth filling. Mathias has recorded that "of the various rotten ways of seeing the New Year in, crouching at the end of a very stuffy mine (so stuffy that the light went out if you held it near the roof), and arranging slabs of guncotton on so that they touched one another, takes the biscuit".

Switch boards were made for the mines, single for 1 and 2, and a combined one for 3, 4, 5 and 6. The mines were tested daily with a galvanometer and the switch boards required constant attention as soon as the weather got damp, as ordinary wire nails, were used as points. Mathias slept by the complicated switch board in C Redoubt.

The energies of the field companies were not of course confined to mining. A great deal of digging of fire and communication trenches went on. 22nd Company ran out a sap from the site of No. 4 blockhouse to form a bombing post on the river front. 17th Company built a number of trench bridges and subsequently widened them. Platforms were made for two naval guns in the palmgroves to deal with an expected boat attack. A good deal of wiring was done, some very near the Turkish trenches where low wire had to be laid, carried out in prepared lengths. On the night of the 28th/29th, Mathias doing this work with Havildar Dalip Singh and some sappers in front of a machine gun post on the site of No. 3 blockhouse, discovered that the Turks had tied ropes to some knife rests across the old road. He cut these and brought in also a packet of propagandist literature left by the Turks.

The 17th Company did most of the odd jobs, besides finding time to improve their own lines and dugouts. Their work included strengthening the high wire entanglement of the second line and adding a low wire entanglement, keeping the pumping station near the Sapper lines working as the river rose and fell, making a shielded observation tower for 82nd Battery, making and flagging gaps in the second line wire in case the reserves had to be rushed forward and work on the Hants Communication Trench.

These "odd jobs" involved the 17th Company in very serious officer casualties. On 17th December, Subadar Baryam Singh was wounded in the abdomen the bullet lodging near his spine. Next day, East, while working on widening trench bridges in the second line, was shot through both lungs. Boyes had already gone to hospital on the 13th with colitis, which kept him there for two months, so Cheshire was transferred from 22nd Company. On the 19th, Crawford was shot through both legs while superintending the digging of a trench from the pump house to the river and on the same night Jemadar Fateh Khan was wounded in the arm. This left the company with only Cheshire and Jemadar Khrishna Bhonsle; so on the 20th, Lieut. K. D. Yearsley, R.E. was posted to command, actually taking over on the 22nd. Of the wounded officers, only Jemadar Fateh Khan, who, though not dangerously wounded, developed pneumonia in hospital, rejoined the company. East died of his wounds in hospital on Christmas Day. He was the son of a celebrated artist. He had been with the company since Basra and his loss was greatly felt by all ranks. Crawford's wounds were septic and he did not recover till after the siege.

The trench mortars made in the R.E. workshops were a great feature in the front line. The original design consisted of two half cylinders of wood, bound together with wire, to form a 30 inch barrel of 3 inch bore. These were mounted on wooden blocks and fired a dynamite bomb by means by a charge of one ounce of black powder ignited by safety fuze through the breech. Their action was a trifle uncertain and often the bomb never left the mortar.

Captain Stace, R.E. then manufactured in his workshops a bomb gun from a Gnome aeroplane engine cylinder. It was mounted on a wooden carriage and could be elevated and depressed, the range being indicated on a dial. The bomb was projected by a charge of half an ounce of black powder and at first a three pound aeroplane bomb was tried; but later a locally manufactured projectile consisting of three sticks of dynamite bound round with large nails and strips of metal and mounted on a wooden base was used. This gun was quite effective up to 200 yards. Sixteen were manufactured and were known as the Kut Babies.

The great event of December was, of course, the Turkish attack on Christmas Eve. The whole of their front line was heavily manned and it is believed that a general attack was intended, but it was actually delivered on the Fort only. At about 7 a.m. a heavy bombardment started and at 11.30 a.m. large numbers of Turks left their trenches and rushed the outer defence of the Fort; but they were held up and eventually driven out by the Bombay Volunteer Artillery, the bombers of the Oxford and Bucks Light Infantry and the 103rd Maharatta Light Infantry. The attack was renewed at 7 p.m. and continued for hours, the position being at times very critical. The brunt was borne by the same troops and the rest of the Oxfords who had come up after the first assault. Later the Norfolks and the 48th Pioneers were brought up and helped to hold the position. At about 3.30 a.m. the Turks, after very heavy losses, gave up the fight: their attempt to take Kut by storm had failed.

The field companies took no part in this action; the mining in the front line continued throughout, the parties being warned to be ready to clear out at a moment's notice.

After this fight it was decided to dig a line of fire trenches from B Redoubt to the river, cutting off the Fort. This was called the Retrenched Line. It was laid out on Christmas night by Major Barker, Captain Tomlinson and Lieut. Spink, who thereby missed their Christmas dinner. It was believed in Kut that the attack had been intended for Christmas Day when the Turks hoped that the British would be more interested in celebration than in defence duties!

During December, little news came from outside. There were few troops in Mesopotamia besides the garrison of Kut, and the Lahore and Meerut Divisions which were known to be on their way from France would take some time to arrive. On the 27th it was announced that General Aylmer was expecting to advance shortly from Ali Gharbi where he had been concentrating. And, on the 29th, one of his aeroplanes flew over Kut and dropped a much needed package of detonators —*two miles outside the defences.*

On the 2nd January, the field companies got their first day of rest during the siege. On this day also the first rain fell.

During the first week of January, 22nd Company laid out and dug, with help from 17th Company, a redoubt at the river end of the Retrenched line. 17th Company wired the Retrenched line. For this they used eight lines of barbed wire coils, prepared in the trench and carried out and fastened down by staples. This plan was suggested by Cheshire and was in fact a local invention of "concertinas".

On the 6th January, one section of 22nd Company started sapping out from between C Redoubt and No. 2 Blockhouse, where the Turks, from a neighbouring sandhill had sapped nearly to our wire and appeared to be mining. An iron sap head plate was made in the R.E. workshops and was used in this sap on the 9th, but was soon riddled with bullets. On the 11th, the sap being then thirty yards out, the last twenty yards was roofed in and the sap head teed. One arm of the T was made into a sentry post with two loopholes and from the other a mine was run towards the sandhill work.

At about 9 p.m. on the 13th the Turks exploded a small mine near the sandhills. Our mining party cleared out very quickly but no damage was done. On the 22nd, after the floods had driven the Turks back, Mathias was able to inspect this mine. The gallery was semi-circular in section and not more than eighteen inches high—not very easy to work in!

On the 5th January a Turkish aeroplane was seen up. It was believed to be an old one captured from us and of little value. On the 7th, heavy gun fire could be heard down stream in the morning, and in the evening it was announced that General Aylmer had captured Shaikh Saad. While the news was welcome, it was a shock of surprise to the garrison that the Turks had commenced their resistance to the relieving force so far down stream.

On the night of the 7th/8th it rained and the trenches and the streets of Kut became pretty filthy; the former in places being feet deep in mud and water. A fairly fine spell followed and the trenches were cleaned up and the "Town Engineers" (late Bridging Train) began to clean up Kut and also to drive covered ways through the houses.

On the 10th it was first noticed that the Turks were beginning to wire round Kut.

On the 13th, the R.E. barge broke loose and floated off down stream. Our gunners tried to sink her but she got away presenting the Turks with valuable stores. They also used her later for a flying bridge at Megassis.

During the middle of the month the field companies had rather a slack time; 17th Company had only minor jobs, including wiring the middle line with concertinas. Jemadar Fathe Khan returned from hospital on the 11th.

The 15th January was a cloudy day and it rained all night and most of the next day. It was very cold and every one was depressed, as it was evident that it would be impossible for the relieving force to move. On the 17th it rained hard all day; the whole of Kut was flooded and the trenches were deep in water. Dams were made round all the mine heads to keep the water out. The river also was rising. The rain went on till 10 a.m. on the 18th. The area between the trenches, especially between C Redoubt and second line where the ground was saucer shaped, was a sheet of water, which was only kept out of the trenches by the parapet and parados. The trenches themselves were knee deep. Soon after dark on the 18th it began raining again, and continued all night; and at 5 a.m. on the 19th, water broke through the parados of the Front Line just behind C Redoubt. A bund (dam) was hastily constructed in the trench just to the east of No. 2 Blockhouse, which prevented the water spreading towards B Redoubt. Mathias just got out of his dugout by the mine switchboard in time, but all the mines were flooded except No. 1 and the new mine from the sap in front of C Redoubt which was on rising ground and in fact was about the only dry place in the area.

Needless to say, the rest of the troops expected the Sappers to provide a panacea for the flooded trenches; but none was forthcoming. No levels had been taken in the Kut peninsula. Matthews suggested draining the flooded area by deepening the middle line trenches down to the river on the east. The Sappers did some work on this plan on the 18th but it was found that a fifteen foot deep trench would be needed. Lift and force pumps were tried but there were not enough for the job; so resort was eventually had to baling with kerosine oil tins; and this was successful though it could only be done at night in the front line. The rain stopped on the 19th and by the 20th, the front and middle lines had been more or less baled dry, but the second line was still flooded.

As a result of the rain, the river had been rising rapidly and by the 20th it was approaching high flood level. The Sappers were put on to the defence of the river ends of the trenches from the middle line rearwards against flood: 17th Company taking the left and 22nd the right of the line. Bunds were built across the trenches on the river bank and also where they cut the Sadd or old Arab bund which encircled the peninsula. Work at both ends was under fire, but there were no casualties.

On the 21st the river reached high flood level and seemed to be still rising. The river edge bunds gave way early in the morning and the 17th Company made a succession of bunds across the trenches to check the water, while the main bunds at the Sadd were being strengthened with puddled walls. The 22nd Company worked at their end all morning. It poured with rain and was bitterly cold. But the Turks must have been equally miserable as they did not even take the trouble to snipe the working parties; and our men could hear the cheering sound of Aylmer's guns down stream.

While our measures against the flood seemed successful, those of the Turks were not. At about 6.30 a.m. on the 21st, a rush of water was seen coming from the west end of the enemy's front line, and as our front line trenches were on a slightly lower level, it poured into them on our left just inside the Sadd. The infantry hastily threw machine guns, ammunition, blankets, etc., over the parados and attempted to check the onrush with bunds; and more bunds were made at the heads of the communication trenches and where these crossed the middle line. The bunds along the first line trench gave way one by one from the left and as each section was flooded its garrison scrambled over the parados. The 22nd Company's mine had to be abandoned hastily and two sappers were killed, shot through the head, in getting back. The flood was checked eventually at a bund on the right of B Redoubt, but the front line west of this and the communication trenches back to the middle line were flooded. The defenders had to get back across the slush to middle line and in doing so some thirty men were killed, mostly among the Gurkhas. Some men were also killed while vacating the trenches and some Gurkhas had been drowned inside them. Picquets were left on the parados of the front line, and when, some hours later, the Turks in their turn were driven from their trenches, these had their revenge, the Gurkhas especially letting the fugitives have it.

All the garrison spent a miserable night, wet through and cold and with no chance of drying anything. Aylmer's guns could be heard down stream but the weather was evidently against him.

On the evacuation of the front line, Matthews went up there to rescue his exploders, and when the Turks left their trenches, he went across and had a good look at their position.

This flood, though disastrous at the time, proved a blessing. It drove the two trench lines well apart and put an end to Turkish attacks. Even the snipers on the right bank got flooded out and for several days it was possible to walk about in the open. Then they got busy again and movement above ground by day became too hazardous.

The period up to 22nd January was a very tiring one. All the troops were wet and cold and there was no hope of drying anything. The trenches were knee deep in water and mud and the streets of Kut nearly as bad.

The morale of the garrison at this period was very good and quite recovered from the retreat. No one dreamed that Kut would not be relieved in a few weeks. The Turks had been fairly quiet since Christmas and the heavy work of trench digging etc. seemed over. Rations were plentiful. Fresh meat had given out on the 26th December and bully beef issued instead. By that day vegetables were very scarce and a small quantity of rice was issued to British troops instead, but this only continued till the end of December, when rice was reserved for the Indian. Firewood became a difficulty in the middle of January, just when the rain made it the more necessary; a systematic survey was made for wood throughout the town. Looting of wood became common; it was taken from trench bridges and wire entanglements and even wooden crosses were stolen from graves. Sentries had to be put on wooden bridges and other structures.

CHAPTER XIII.

Defence of Kut-Al-Amara.
Second Phase—Defence Against Flood.

On the 22nd January, the river had begun to fall; it was a bright sunny day and it was possible to dry clothes and blankets and work was begun on strengthening the new front.

It was at first intended to abandon the whole front line including the Fort, but on 26th January it was decided to hold it from B Redoubt, eastwards. Work was therefore started on the 27th on a trench from just east of B Redoubt to near where Reserve communication trench crossed the middle line. This was called the Echelon Trench. Westward from this, the new foremost line of defence was the Middle Line.

Piquets were established inside C and D Redoubts in the old front line and 17th Company wired these in on the night of 22nd/23rd. On the same night, 22nd Company commenced a high command breastwork between the Sadd and the river on the left of the middle line and just behind the flooded trench. This was 150 yards long and four feet six inches high, and revetted with a puddled clay wall one foot thick. It was laid in two layers, and as one third of the length could be done each night it was completed on the 28th, one night (23rd/24th) having been lost owing to heavy rain, under which the fresh puddle wall would not stand.

From the 23rd to the 28th, 17th Company put up a high wire entanglement along the middle line and worked also on the front line, strengthening the wire round B Redoubt and eastwards. Wiring material was getting scarce and it was now necessary to collect the wire and pickets from old obstacles.

After the 23rd the weather improved. The night temperature had fallen to just above freezing point.

On the 28th, one section of 22nd Company put up a new observation tower for 104th Heavy Battery. This was a three legged structure; one of the legs being a tall palm tree whose fronds concealed the actual platform on which a wagon shield was fixed. This observatory was never spotted by the enemy. On the 30th, 22nd Company repaired the brick kilns observatories, which had been damaged by shells.

On the 21st, Gen. Aylmer had been repulsed at Hanna; the attack had been made across a sea of mud and the casualties had been very heavy. Kut was full of rumours and, on the 26th, Gen. Townshend issued a communique, in which he explained his reasons for standing at Kut and his confidence of early relief.

Rations were nevertheless reduced to three quarter scale on the 24th and horse meat was issued to British troops, including of course our British officers. As a whole, the officers were agreeably surprised. White bread was also no longer issued to the troops after the 28th, but reserved for hospitals. Brown bread, which was quite good at first but deteriorated as the proportion of coarse flour increased, was issued instead. Sugar gave out about the same time.

On the 24th, Major Winsloe, R.E., the Field Engineer, was wounded in the leg. It was not a serious wound but the bullet could not be found and he remained a cripple during the siege; Major Barker took over his work.

On the 28th, Matthews, who had been seedy for some days with what looked like turning into dysentery, went into Kut and stayed in the D.E.C's. house for a rest till 4th February, when he returned much better.

From 31st January to 3rd February, both companies had a slack time. 17th Company put up an observation tower in the palm groves south of the town and both companies cleaned up their bivouacs and completed a communication trench from the bivouac to the junction of 67th communication trench and the second line; which was most useful in getting to work.

The weather was beautiful but very cold at night, the thermometer showing eleven degrees of frost. It must be remembered that nearly everyone was in khaki drill and few had more than one blanket. There was no straw and the men slept on the bare ground. Much might doubtless have been done to improve matters but everyone was expecting early relief.

In the afternoon, officers used to walk into Kut and see friends in hospital, or visit the D.E.C's. headquarters which were in two houses near the river. The D.E.C. had a real fire place and his mess was very hospitable and gave visitors tea as long as there was any to give. There was also a shooting gallery on the roof whence a shot could be taken at enemy snipers, 800 yards away, across the river. Here also the latest news and rumours could be heard and discussed.

On the 4th February, Matthews came back from the D.E.C's. house, and on the 5th, Mathias went there for a rest. Boyes also came on a visit from hospital on the 4th, still looking very ill.

During the 4th, 5th and 6th, both companies were employed on the echelon trench, and they also dug a series of wells behind the echelon trench and the old middle line. These were for use in the new flood control. They were 20 feet wide, and had a berm three feet wide six feet below the surface, connected by a communication trench with the trenches.

The flood protection scheme was issued cn the 7th. Spink had been taking levels since 30th January. There was actually no proper levelling instrument in Kut, and he had to improvise but he borrowed an artillery director from a battery and used it very successfully. Floods were expected about 15th March from the melting of the snow in Armenia but they might come earlier. Actually the Kut garrison used to receive twelve days warning of floods from our liaison officer with the Russians operating round the head waters of the Tigris.

In the Kut peninsula the ground falls away from the river, and the normal protection is the Arab bund or Sadd following the river bank and connecting with the sandhills at the base of the peninsula; but the Turks held the sandhills and so could flood the peninsula. The greatest depression lay round the left half of the middle line.

The flood protection work ordered was :—

A. The Sadd round from the left of the middle line to the Fort to be strengthened and heightened. This was done by Arab coolies under Lieut. Abbott. They were a trifle gunshy but eventually did good work.

B. The parapet of the fire trenches from the left of the middle line, along the middle line, echelon trench and front line, to the Fort to be converted into a four feet six inches high breastwork revetted by a wall of puddled clay one foot thick.

C. A bund to be made all round the Fort and an inner "keep" bund to be made inside. A bund was also to be built on the west side of River communication trench from the Fort to middle line, to prevent River communication trench and the Fort cart road being flooded. This bund could be used as a causeway if necessary.

D. As levels showed that the floods might top the middle line breastwork at its centre, an inner bund was built from the middle line between Hants and 67th communication trenches looping behind second line and then back to middle line. This was made by the 48th Pioneers.

Matthews was in engineer charge of the flood protection in the north-west section, i.e. along the middle line to its junction with echelon trench. The infantry did the work. 22nd Company put up picket and string profiles all along the front, raising them to show each night's task. The British battalion was supposed not to be able to puddle clay, so the 22nd Company built their revetment wall for them. The 22nd Company officers had; of course, to control the infantry's work as well as their own.

Both companies worked principally on the breastworks till the end of February. It was found that the work of revetting the traverses was particularly slow at night; so from the 17th February, the breastworks were built straight, and when they were high enough to conceal work on the traverses, the latter were continued by day. As a result the work on the traverse revetments went twice as fast and was of better quality. Yearsley put up in some places pairs of overlapping mud brick walls, six feet high, as a substitute for traverses; this saved having to get down into the wet trench.

On the 11th, 22nd Company commenced a seven foot high wall of pise work on the left of the middle line at the Sadd, to defilade workers in the neighbourhood. On the 14th, 17th Company began to build another seven foot wall where the inner bund left the middle line, in order to screen an exit for guns at this point. There was a good deal of rivalry between the companies as to these walls. The rain would not allow the mud to set and small lengths of each wall were apt to collapse to the amusement of the other company. 17th Company reinforced their walls with buttresses.

On the earthwork of the bunds, tasks of ten cubic feet per man were found suitable. The earth had to be carried, of course, from borrow pits well away from the toe of the breastwork.

The 22nd Company finished their wall on the 23rd. The middle line breastwork was then three feet high. On the 24th, an experiment was tried of erecting a screen of reed mats before dawn and working behind them by day. These attracted some fire but not enough to stop work which improved greatly in quality and quantity.

It rained hard on the 9th and 10th February, but after that it was fairly fine, with occasional showers, till the end of the month; though each shower left a legacy of mud. After the 14th the nights got warmer and, towards the end of the month, flies became a nuisance.

Mathias came back from his rest cure at the D.E.C's. on the 11th, and Boyes came back from hospital on the 13th. The Kut hospitals were most depressing places and far more dangerous than the trenches. Sick and wounded used to leave hospital as early as possible and men who had lost a limb were often found in the trenches. On Boyes's return to 17th Company, Cheshire went back to 22nd.

The wells made by the two companies which were an important factor in the work gave a good deal of trouble, as they were always falling in at the bottom. Linings were eventually made for them of corrugated sheet iron strutted into position.

On the 12th began the first regular "hymn of hate" from the Turkish guns, which from this time on opened fire regularly about 4 p.m. and continued till dusk. Their fire at the town was in the nature of browning but they made quite good practice at the batteries. The proximity of the 82nd and 104th Batteries made the sapper bivouacs very unhealthy and the companies used to vacate them at 4 p.m. and go into middle line till it was time to go on to the night's work.

On 13th February, an enemy aeroplane made three trips over Kut and dropped bombs. Everyone with a rifle blazed away at it but without result. Anti-aircraft measures were ordered and consisted of mounting four machine guns on barrels on the roof of 18th Brigade headquarters and a thirteen pounder with sunk trail in the space behind the sapper bivouac. The aeroplane came back on the 19th and the 13 pounder got off some rounds at it, but it had a traverse of only 90 degrees and when two Turkish aeroplanes came over next day, they avoided its arc. They were using our own aeroplane bombs from the R.N.A.S. barge abandoned at Umm-Al-Tubul.

Matthews now evolved a new anti-aircraft gun mounting which was erected by the 22nd Company on the 21st and 22nd. It consisted of a mahela mast sunk into a wood-lined pit with hard wood bearings to hold it vertical. The axle of the 13 pounder was fastened, strutted and stayed to the top of the mast and the trail moved in a circular pit with floor and outer wall of wood. The sappers also made special fittings for the sights to give both the horizontal and vertical gun layers a wide field of view. This mounting was a great success, Matthews and his men watched the first shot with some misgivings, but the mounting stood and the shell very nearly got the aeroplane. After practice, the gunners used to get off as much as five rounds at an aeroplane per trip and the Turks admitted two hits.

On the 17th February, the Turks first used "Flatulent Flossie," the ancient bronze mortar which 22nd Company had not destroyed at Ctesiphon. It never did any harm but the fragments of the bomb were in great demand as ash trays, etc.

On the 18th, the Turks were absolutely silent in their lines. An attack was suspected and troops slept fully equipped, but nothing happened.

On the 21st, on return from work about 11.30 p.m., the companies found secret orders awaiting them. It appeared that Gen. Aylmer was attacking at dawn and the Kut garrison was to make a sortie to assist them at 7 a.m. next day. 22nd Company were ordered to make two trench bridges for artillery between A and B Redoubts. Mathias and one section constructed these during the night. Everything was ready at 7 a.m. At 6 a.m. very heavy gun fire was heard down stream. The troops waited till 2.30 p.m. when it was announced that fighting was improbable, and at 3.45 p.m. they stood down. There had been no attack at Hanna after all. On the 26th, Mathias went out and removed his bridges again.

Other work done by the 17th Company during the month included repairs to 450 yards of the wire from which all the pickets had been stolen, repairs and improvements to wire in several other places, erecting two new bridges for guns over the second line and keeping the pumping station near the bivouac in order during the rise and fall of the river.

Since the repulse at Hanna, all rations, except meat, had been reduced to three quarter scale. The officers' mess were still doing fairly well with their stores. Arab shops and hawkers were still selling tinned milk, tea coffee, salt, cigarettes, etc., but the prices were very high. Kabobs, i.e. small pancakes fried in fat were also sold in the bazar, and were greatly appreciated. They became scarce at the end of February when the price had risen to a rupee each and disappeared in the middle of March. Milk, sugar and butter had disappeared from the rations by 10th February. There was still some jam in the bazar, for which Rs. 12 a tin was asked. At an auction of a deceased officer's kit on 9th February, the following prices were obtained :—

  100 cigarettes ... ... Rs. 100.
  ½ lb. Army and Navy mixture tobacco ... Rs. 49.
  ½ lb. tin of butter ... ... Rs. 12.
  1 bottle whiskey ... ... Rs. 75.
  1 lb. sugar ... ... Rs. 20.

On the 27th the Sapper and Miner mess gave a dinner to Col. Wilson and Capt. Tomlinson, when they came to inspect the work. As the mess expected early relief, they were lavish with stores and the following dinner is remembered as the last good meal up to November, 1918 :—

Soup—Mule.
Fish—Sardines on toast.
Joint—Horsepie with tinned peas and beans.
Sweet—Appletart (Morton's apple rings) and cream (Ideal
    milk and flour).
Cheese straws.
Coffee and dessert (dates).

By the 10th February firewood ceased to be issued except to hospital. The troops cooked with crude oil on cookers manufactured in the R.E. workshops. The Sapper and Miner officers were sometimes able to get hold of some wood from works and used to seize the opportunity to take it into the D.E.C's. house and have a hot bath.

One or more of our aeroplanes flew over Kut every day and dropped messages, papers, etc. The relief force aeroplanes were of an obsolete pattern and occasionally used to drop valuable packages outside the area. It was grasped by the garrison that the repulse at Hanna had involved very heavy losses and that Gen. Aylmer would have to wait for reinforcements. The Lahore Division was moving up, and on the 7th February it was announced in a communique that the 13th (British) Division was coming from Egypt, but the garrison estimated it would be six weeks before it could arrive.

By the end of February the Indian troops were getting practically norations except coarse barley flour. On the

22nd, General Townshend issued a communique asking the Mussalmans to eat horse flesh. Had a definite order been issued, it would probably have been obeyed. The O.Cs. of two Indian battalions (103rd Mahratta Light Infantry and 2nd/7th Gurkha Rifles) issued such an order and these two battalions obeyed it. But Gen. Townshend would not issue a general order. Opinions had been wirelessed from eminent Hindu and Mussalman leaders in India that the eating of horse flesh was permissible under the circumstances; but the sepoys believed that such an opinion would not be accepted in the villages and that their compliance would lead to their being ostracised on their return. The Sappers and Miners got a little rice in addition to the barley, but by the end of the month their working capacity was down to a half, and a four hour relief was as much as they could manage.

Scurvy also started among the Indian troops owing to lack of vegetables, and, by the end of February, a company could not produce a working party of more than 80 men, including sapper drivers who were now put on to digging.

On the 27th February, Matthews got up a sweepstake in the garrison on the date of relief. Tickets were five rupees and the date fixed was when the first steamer of the relief force passed the Fort. The favourite dates were in the latter half of March. Gen. Melliss drew the High Field (denominated Mosul) and Matthews hesitated to inform him for fear of being told off as a pessimist; but on the last day of the siege he had to hand over the prize of Rs. 550 to the general.

Grass was used for food when vegetables failed. At first this had disastrous results but the P.M.O. issued instructions as to which grasses were edible and which were poisonous. At the end of February grass was getting scarce and by the middle of March it could no longer be found.

During the first week in March, work continued on the bunds; the sappers working both by day and night. On the 6th, 17th Company worked on a new communication trench running south from the east end of second line.

March started with a heavy bombardment on the 1st from 4 p.m. to 6.15 p.m. Three Turk aeroplanes came over at the same time and, besides bombing, spotted for their guns. Not much damage was done, but one bomb went through the roof of the officers' hospital in Kut and failed to explode, while another scored a direct hit on Cheshire's "funk pit" a few minutes after he had left it.

On the 2nd, the Turks started a new trick with high angle rifle fire. It was irritating but not very effective.

The river started rising again and on 4th March had reached flood level but it subsided again. The weather was fine.

On the 5th March, our observers saw large cylinders being unloaded at Shumran. A gas attack was expected and improvised gas masks were issued; but no gas attack ever came.

On the 6th a very heavy bombardment was heard down stream, and about 4 p.m. on the 7th, Yearsley and Matthews were called into Kut to receive orders. They were told that Gen. Aylmer was going to make a night march on the right bank and attack the Essin position at the Dujailah Redoubt next morning. The Kut garrison was to cooperate. Gen. Delamain and the 16th Brigade were to hold the trenches. Gen. Melliss and a landing force were to be ferried across the river by the Samana to a point just east of the Hai, whence he was to clear the right bank as far as opposite the Fort. 17th and 22nd Companies and the Sirmur Sappers were to be on the right of the second line by 7 a.m. on the 8th, ready to construct two flying bridges to ferry the rest of the force across. The material was to be brought down from the R.E. headquarters by the Bridging Train on rafts towed by a lauch and as soon as it arrived, 17th Company was to cross and commence operations.

On the night of the 7th/8th an attempt was made to destroy the enemy's bridge across the Hai by a mine floated down from Woolpress. The attempt failed.

On the 8th, the two companies left their bivouac at 6.30 a.m. and went to the communication trench which 17th Company had dug on the 6th. There followed a long day of waiting and disappointment. In the morning, heavy fire was heard from the Dujailah Redoubt and shells could be seen bursting all over it. Turkish troops could also be seen moving up, but our men were forbidden to fire as the crossing was to be a surprise. In the afternoon, Matthews went into Kut for news and heard that Aylmer had failed to get through, but would attack again. In the afternoon the artillery fire to the east rose to a great intensity but at 5.30 p.m. it ceased; and it was evident that the attack had again failed.

Food was sent out to the companies and the officers, still full of hope, ate their last tin of pineapple!

The Sappers knew that the Lahore Division had been engaged and that their comrades of the 20th and 21st Companies must be involved in the fight they had been listening to ; but the 17th Company was spared the knowledge that their old commander, Capt. Arbuthnot had been killed leading a party of the Manchesters in the last desperate fight in the redoubt.

The two companies remained in the trench till 12.30 p.m. on the 9th, when they were ordered back to the lines. Everyone now knew that Aylmer had failed and retreated, and there was great depression throughout the garrison. There were also rumours of a further reduction in rations.

The story of the night march on Dujailah (brilliantly led by Capt. K. Mason, R.E., 20th Company, 3rd Sappers and Miners), of the delay while the artillery bombarded the almost empty position and of the desperate infantry attacks when the Turks had brought up their best troops, is well known. Much discussion took place in Kut as to whether the crossing of the river by the garrison while the fight was in progress would have just turned the scale or resulted in the annihilation of the troops that crossed.

On the 10th March the expected orders about rations were issued. The bread ration for British troops was reduced to ten ounces ; the jam issue finally ceased, though a minute quantity of butter was issued biweekly for a short time. Meat was still plentiful as the Indians would not eat it. 25 horses and mules were killed for meat daily and 900 were now set aside for this purpose; while 417 were at once destroyed to save grain, including all chargers. The only foodstuffs that were plentiful were tea, coffee and salt. In the officers' mess stores, there only remained a little jam, flour, oatmeal and curry powder and a few tins of bully beef.

Gen. Townshend issued a communique this day, repeating Gen. Aylmer's telegram to him and urging the garrison to be patient as relief would surely come. The Turks sent in proposing surrender, which the General of course refused.

Mosquitoes began to appear this day.

On the evening of the 10th March, the Sappers again worked on the middle line bund. On the 11th, 17th Company laid out a small redoubt in the echelon trench which the 48th Pioneers dug and the company wired on this and the two succeeding nights. Apart from this, both companies worked on the middle line bund from four to six hours every night, partly reinforcing weak spots and partly putting in cores of puddled clay where fire or communication trenches crossed the bunds. These cores were keyed into the sides and bottoms of the trenches and much labour would have been saved if they had been thought of before.

It rained on 11th March and at 8 a.m. on the 12th there was a terrific thunderstorm. Many of the dugouts were flooded out and the trenches were in an awful state. The sappers had to spend some time cleaning out their bivouac besides their night work. The rain brought forth myriads of small frogs, which made progress down any trench a messy business. The rain damaged a number of traverses in the middle line which had to be built up again.

14th March was a very fine day; the river was rising fast. On the 15th it was over the level of 21st January. After dinner, Matthews went across and looked at the river ends (on the west) of our old front line and the old Turkish front line. He found that flood water was coming in fast at both trench ends. On the 16th, though the river level fell a little, the flood water reached the middle line at its junction with 67th communication trench and filled up the borrow pits. On the 17th it continued to rise and also broke into B Redoubt where the piquet post had to be abandoned. 22nd Company fixed a gauge at the lowest portion of middle line (between reserve and 67th communication trench) and found six inches of water there this day.

On the 19th, Matthews, who had been seedy some days with suspected enteric, went into hospital. Yearsley took over charge of the flood protection in the north-west section and 17th Company took over engineer charge generally of that section, 22nd Company taking over general work.

Mathias, on 17th March, had laid out a reserve bund in front of 82nd Battery's position, connecting the Sadd with the inner bund. The 48th Pioneers commenced building this on the 19th and 17th Company strengthened its junction with the Sadd.

On the 20th, the river was still falling; the snipers on the right bank who had retired when the flood came, returned and made themselves a nuisance again. The companies were employed on raising the parapets of various communication trenches to keep surface water out, filling in the communication trenches for some distance in front of the middle line. 17th Company also did some wire repairs and added an extra line of high wire entanglement in front of middle line opposite Hants communication trench.

On the 21st, the flood was slightly down. The 22nd Company this day commenced building three pise work walls seven feet high, to defilade the crossing of Hants communication trench and the reserve bund. These were built in one foot layers and stood well.

On the 23rd, the river began to rise again, though no big flood was expected; but at nightfall it had reached previous high level and the gauge showed six inches of water.

At 1 p.m. on the 24th, Mathias got an urgent message from the D.E.C. to go to the help of Spink, who was Assistant Field Engineer in the north-east section. He went off with three sections. The previous evening water had come into the front line trench near B Redoubt and the check bunds made by the infantry in the trench between it and A Redoubt gave way. The onrush of water was checked by a bund which had been made by the Sirmur Sappers to the east of A Redoubt but the latter had to be abandoned. At 9 p.m. on the 23rd, the bund at the front line end of retrenched line gave way and Spink only just managed to prevent the flood entering Gurkha communication trench towards middle line. By doing so, he saved the situation as the bund at the junction of middle line and Gurkha communication trench was weak. The 22nd Company immediately got to work at this weak point, putting in a puddled core and filling in the trench behind and stamping the earth well down. By dawn on the 24th they had made it safe and returned to their bivouac.

During the day (24th), a subsidence was also noticed on the slope of the revetment on the site of the old north-west section headquarters which had been filled in, and the 17th Company, assisted by the 22nd Company and parties of the 104th and 117th, worked by reliefs from 5 p.m. till 11.30 p.m., adding earth to the firing step in the centre 21 bays. The right half of 17th Company who had been on the first relief were called out soon after their return to bivouac to deal with a leak in the Sudd behind the left of the middle line, which they rectified by 12.30 a.m. During this night also, the 17th Company pegged down "chittai" mats on the toe of the breastwork to protect it from wave action.

At 7 a.m. on the 25th, the flood gauge showed 19 inches of water and the parapet was getting scoured; signs of percolation appeared in a section of the middle line and so the bottom of the trench was filled in to a depth of 12 inches with rammed earth. By the evening, all was safe again. This was the most anxious period of the flood control. Yearsley slept near the breastwork and had to be continually watching it ; and the sappers, with short periods for meals and sleep, were kept on work till the position was secure.

On the following nights, the 22nd Company continued their screen walls begun on the 21st and these were completed on the 28th.

On the 26th and 27th, the flood subsided slowly. On the 26th, when a strong north wind was driving waves against the breastwork, an experiment was tried of pouring crude oil on the water, but the effect was small. The 17th Company put down more chittai mats. On the 27th, Yearsley and Mathias took levels and found that the river flood outside the west end of middle line was three feet higher than that against the middle of the line. During a later flood, the 22nd Punjabis, at the request of the D.E.C., made a reconnaissance in the sand-hills and found that the water was running away through a gap in them.

The flood on the 24th had almost isolated the Fort and from the 25th to the 28th, 22nd Company was ordered to supply a section daily to assist in the north-east section. This reduced the company by half, as the men got very little rest during their 24 hours and had to be rested the next day.

While the fight against the flood was going on, the enemy's artillery and snipers were active. Enemy aeroplanes came over on the morning of the 18th March and again at dusk when they bombed Kut and hit the British General Hospital, inflicting 32 casualties. The same day their guns tried to sink the Samana. The next day they tried again and hit her twice, once in the funnel and once by a very lucky shot cutting the main steam joint. This was a three way connection to take a pressure of 180 pounds and it was generally believed that the Samana was finished ; but Stace designed a fitting from piping and odds and ends, and Sergt. Toleman made it—a job requiring a real artist at his trade. As a result, the Samana could still do its ferry work, though at reduced speed, and Woolpress could still be held. She was now moored behind a barge on which a double wall of kerosene oil tins, filled with earth, was erected by the 48th Pioneers. During its erection, Sapper Indar Singh plunged into the river to rescue a pioneer who had been wounded.

On the night of the 20th, a Turkish aeroplane dropped four incendiary bombs. The only one that ignited fell in open country.

On the 22nd, there was a heavy bombardment from 5.45 a.m. to 9.15 a.m. with aeroplane observation, and again from 5.30 p.m. to 7 p.m. This was the heaviest bombardment since the fighting period of the siege and about 2,000 shells were thrown into Kut. Not much damage was done, our casualties being two killed and 15 wounded, but these included one sapper killed and one with his leg blown off—both in the R.E. workshops. The two field companies took cover in the second line. More incendiary bombs were dropped but no harm was done. There was another bombardment next day; and on both these days an attack was expected and the troops slept fully equipped; but nothing happened. On the 23rd our five inch guns took on two eight inch Turkish naval guns which had been mounted above Kut. They looked so enormous and conspicuous that it was at first thought they were dummies. Our guns knocked them both out.

Meanwhile the food shortage grew more intense. On 18th March, the bread ration was reduced from 10 to 8 ounces, and the Indian ration of coarsely ground barley flour was reduced from 12 to 10 ounces. The bread ration was made from a mixture of fine flour and "atta." Attempts to make it with barley flour failed. The barley was ground in Kut in mills rigged up by Capt. Wingfield Smith, R.F.C., with two engines, one of which also drove a dynamo to light headquarters. The engines were kept in repair with " spares " dropped by our aeroplanes, but many repairs were also done in R.E. workshops. The grindstones were always breaking, but our workshops kept them going by shrinking on wheel tyres. Two small stones were also dropped by aeroplanes and others cut from stones of local donkey mills. The engine fuel just lasted out the siege.

The Indian sappers tried to supplement their rations by cornstalks; these were cleaned and cut up small and mixed with the flour. Some palm trees were also cut down for the juice in the trunks, but this was soon prohibited; but if a tree was blown down by a shell, there was a rush for it. Smokers felt the lack of tobacco severely, and some tried to smoke orange leaves; but the Arabs complained that their trees were being destroyed and this too was prohibited.

On the 23rd the Sapper and Miner mess had a windfall. Matthews returned from hospital though still too seedy for work. He remembered that he had in his dugout two parcels for Campbell and Garrett. These were now opened and found to contain, among other things, some acid drops, some chocolate, 48 packets of consolidated soup and 12 tins of condensed milk. This find was very cheering.

On the 24th, the supplies issued the last of their delicacies—a little pineapple, rice, vinegar and lime juice. Dates, which had been issued when sugar failed, also ran out this day. The mess stock of oatmeal finally ran out on the 28th.

At the end of March everyone was feeling the food shortage; there was not much actual sickness, though more than formerly and no actual pangs of hunger : but everyone was weak. The soles of the feet hurt if you walked or stood, the shoulders and back if you lay down and the seat if you sat. Half the officers felt a craving for alcohol and the other half for sweets. Cheshire's particular desire was for Worcestershire Sauce.

Still everyone was optimistic and expected relief. War diaries and summaries of engineer work were prepared. It was known that General Gorringe had replaced General Aylmer in command of the relieving force; and there was speculation as to whether his well known drive would break through or break itself against impregnable positions. The sound of his guns downstream could be heard continually and our aeroplanes flew over every day. It was understood that Gorringe was waiting for the 13th Division.

The weather at the latter half of March had been good—and much warmer. Flies had become a very serious nuisance.

CHAPTER XIV.

The Last Month.

The last month of the siege provides a story of ever lessening rations, of hopes raised and deferred and of flood protection work by men who grew weaker every day. The wind was a very important factor. If it was in the south, there was little danger from the floods, but it was likely to bring rain, and hamper the relief force; if in the north, the floods were dangerous but Gorringe might be able to attack.

On 29th March, it was decided to widen the parapet along the worst four hundred yards of the middle line where it had been washed away. All earth had to be carried from borrow pits behind the trenches. Both companies helped the infantry with this on the nights of 29th/30th and 30th/31st. On the 31st it was cloudy all day and a little rain fell, which at 9 p.m. developed into a terrific thunderstorm and stopped the companies which were again on the middle line. The trenches and dugouts got into an awful state and the next day had to be spent in cleaning up the bivouacs.

On 1st April the Indian ration was reduced to 10 ounces of barley meal, four ounces of barley for parching and one third of an ounce of ghi.

The bread ration was baked in 12 ounce loaves. A great discovery had been made that mule fat could be boiled down into dripping and used as butter. All the food in the officers' mess was divided very carefully into five parts for each meal. Grass was now very difficult to find, very coarse and almost inedible.

The thunderstorm on the 31st flooded 30th Communication Trench. Someone had taken earth from the spoil banks to strengthen the middle line breastwork and the surface water of the storm rushed in. Nothing could be done to remedy this.

On the 2nd April, the ground began to dry but on the 3rd at 4 p.m., there was a very heavy hail storm, with hailstones up to three quarters of an inch in diameter. The 4th was a beautiful day, but the river began to rise rapidly. The sappers kept a water patrol on the Sadd (no such patrol of course was needed on the breastwork); but the wind in the palm trees often sounded like water pouring through a breach and the officers frequently hurried out at night to investigate this— which always turned out to be a false alarm.

On the 4th, both companies worked strengthening weak places on the Sadd.

On the 5th, a heavy bombardment was heard downstream in the early morning and at 9 a.m. it was announced that General Gorringe had captured the first line of the Hannah position. The garrison was held in readiness to carry out scheme B—a sortie from the front line. The sappers took up all trench bridges which had been issued to help in widening the middle line breastwork and returned them to the 48th Pioneers who held them normally for tactical purposes. Everyone was very hopeful.

Matthews resumed command of 22nd Company this day.

On the morning of the 7th a communique was issued to the effect that Gorringe had captured the whole of Hannah and Falahiyah positions and had dug in within four hundred yards of the Sunnaiyat position. This sounded very hopeful; it was not known that the Turks had not seriously defended Hannah nor anticipated that Sunnaiyat would not be stormed for 10 months.

There was no work this day, the troops standing by for a sortie. The gauge stood at one foot nine inches. There was again no work on the 8th; the flood was one inch higher.

On the 8th April, the bread ration was six ounces and, on the 9th, it was reduced to five ounces; and at the same time the Indian ration of barley was reduced from ten ounces to seven and the four ounces for parching ceased. This was all that the men were getting.

Kerosine oil issues had stopped. The Sapper and Miner mess had a small stock, which provided a light in the mess for twenty minutes during dinner and each officer had five minutes light in his dugout when he turned in.

On the 10th, percolation, which had been bad in part of the middle line, looked like getting out of control. Both companies and 70 pioneers worked by reliefs, in the afternoon, filling in the trench here. The men could only work a 90 minute relief and they were very weak; it was pitiful seeing them try to dig.

Heavy firing was heard downstream in the morning and about 2 p.m. General Townshend issued a communique that came as a bad shock : the relief force had been repulsed from Sunnaiyat and the general considered there was no hope of relief by the 15th, the day that he had calculated his rations for. Rations were therefore to be reduced to five ounces of flour a meal for all troops. This meant a four ounce loaf of bread for the British. It was hoped that this ration would last till the 21st. The communique ended with a strong appeal to Indians to eat horse flesh.

On the 6th, the garrison stood to arms at 5.30 a.m. in anticipation of operations but nothing happened. The river was still rising and had risen 27 feet since the low water level at Christmas. The middle line flood gauge showed one foot and seven and a half inches at 9 p.m. During the night the 17th Company refixed the mats along the middle line breastwork and the 22nd Company worked at communication trench and trench junctions.

On the 11th, another communique was issued corroborating that the Relief Force could not advance at once. On this day, Subedar Muhammad Din said that he would give the company a lead in eating horse flesh, but the men were still doubtful.

At 2 p.m. on the 12th the General had all C.Os. and Indian officers of Indian units up to discuss the horsemeat question. He said that although the men must decide for themselves, they must understand that those who refused meat would forfeit all hope of promotion. The Muhammadans told the general that they would start eating horsemeat at once but they drew the line at mule. Apparently their objections had been partly based on the fear that the horses might have had connection with donkeys.

The weather looked threatening though there was not much rain. The 17th Company put down more mats on the breastwork and the 22nd Company and the Pioneers went on filling in the bad parts of the middle line trenches.

On the 13th April, all the sappers except a few Brahmans in 22nd Company decided to eat horsemeat. Gen. Townshend had issued an opinion of the A.D.M.S. that this was absolutely necessary to preserve health and even life. The Mahrattas and Sikhs of the 17th Company asked that a company order should be issued to salve their consciences.

The decision came too late: the men were so weak that the meat did them little good. It was also accompanied by a tragedy. A young Sikh lance naik of the 22nd Company committed suicide rather than comply with it. He was one of Matthews' bridge demolition party of December and had been awarded the Indian Order of Merit.

On the 14th there was a south-east gale with rain at intervals. Yearsley and Matthews tried to kill fish with gun-cotton, but the snipers on the right bank were too active. The garrison of Woolpress had managed to get fish throughout the siege.

On the 15th, the flood gauge showed one foot five and a half inches. The companies worked on the middle line where percolation mostly from below was troublesome. An officer of the 117th had fixed kerosine oil tins in sumps in his part of the line; the water drained into these and could then be thrown out.

9,500 Indian troops were eating horse meat this day. A very distinguished Indian officer of an infantry regiment was removed from his battalion for discouraging it.

Days were dragging terribly now. There was little work, as the men were too weak to do more than three quarters of an hour. It was impossible to walk for more than a mile without getting tired, and no one cared to do anything that might induce an appetite.

A communique on the 15th announced that the relief force had taken part of the Bait Aessa position on the right bank.

The 16th was fine and quite warm; and mosquitoes were now very bad. Food from aeroplanes was first dropped this day. The 48th Pioneers had marked an area near the brick-kilns, and a fatigue party with mules was stationed there. Six aeroplanes dropped food this day. One 100 pound bag of flour fell on a sepoy and killed him and one bag of sugar fell outside in the flooded area and was retrieved that night by a volunteer party of the 66th.

There was quite a heavy bombardment in the evening.

On the 17th heavy gun fire was heard down stream on the right bank, and at 5 p.m. it was announced that the Lahore division had captured the rest of Bait Aessa.

The river had risen again and the flood gauge stood at eighteen inches. Both companies were out this night putting corrugated sheet iron and mats on the breastwork.

The bread ration was reduced this day to four ounces; this provided a loaf about three inches by two and one third of an inch thick, "a silly looking little thing, and very solid; a lot of barley flour was mixed with wheat flour, resulting in a stodgy brown loaf with a lot of husk in it". Besides this there was absolutely nothing left except horseflesh.

A Turkish flag of truce came in to say that if any more Arabs tried to leave Kut they would be fired on. The Arabs in the town were starving, the women and children especially suffering. Many tried to get away and continued doing so to the end, especially by swimming, but the Turkish river piquets shot them unmercifully.

More food was dropped by aeroplanes this day.

During the night of the 17th/18th very heavy rifle and machine gun fire was heard downstream; which was explained next afternoon by the news of the repulse of the great Turkish counterattack at Bait Aessa. The enemys' losses were reported to be very large and the garrison thought that after this holocaust, the Turks could not have resisted a further advance on the right bank—a view which was shared by many officers of the relieving force and by the Turks themselves.

Subedar Baryam Singh died this night. He had been dangerously wounded in December but had seemed to be getting on well till the middle of March; when he relapsed and in the end just faded away. He was amazingly cheerful and when Brigadier General Evans used to visit him asked him to wireless to his family not to worry. He was a very fine old gentleman and maintained his courtesy and uncomplaining attitude to the end.

Baryam Singh got his I.O.M. in 1900 as a naik when he, Lieut. J. B. Corry and Sapper Nur Mohammad were decorated for gallantry at the storm of Nodiz Fort in Mekran. All these three were killed in the Great War.

The river, on the 18th, rose above all previous levels; the flood gauge showed twenty two inches, but began to go down at night. Next day the wind went to the north-east, and the flood against the middle line rose to two feet two and a half inches with waves up to two feet seven and a half inches. 22nd Company helped 17th Company to carry out more mats and corrugated sheet iron, which 17th Company fixed. This two hours work left the men quite exhausted.

The Turks were now taking notice of our food dropping aeroplanes and put up a barrage against them; and one of our machines was driven down by a Turk.

The wind remained in the north, but the flood protection had stood the test and gave no more anxiety. On the 22nd both companies put down more corrugated sheet iron and wood salved from trench bridges on the breastwork. This was the last bund work. The ground, however, was getting very water logged and dugouts had to be filled in.

On the 20th, a further communique was issued about Bait Aessa. When the full story of the Turkish losses was known every one was sure that relief was coming at last. But on the 23rd came the news of another disastrous repulse at Sunniayat; this was the last news heard of the relieving force and everyone realised that there was little hope.

Sickness was now increasing fast and the death rate was rising. The normal temperature of the garrison had fallen to 96 degrees and the pulse to 55 and there was a great decrease in weight. The Indian troops looked mere skeletons and the sights in the Indian hospitals were dreadful.

The last normal siege rations were issued on the 21st. There remained one full day's reserve rations and the emergency rations. Each of these were to last two days. Most of the troops had eaten their real emergency rations at Ctesiphon and had drawn normal rations instead. The reserve rations were issued on the 22nd and 23rd and the men rejoiced in getting eight ounces of flour. The officers tried to suppliment their rations by husking forage oats to make porridge but the process was too laborious.

On 24th April the aeroplane rations were issued for the first time; they lasted four days. The British got 4 oz. white bread, one oz. sugar, ½ oz. chocolate and ⅛ oz. salt; the Indian 4 oz. flour, 1 oz. goor, ½ oz. dhal and ⅛ oz. salt. The bread and chocolate looked so good that it was difficult not to eat it straight off.

During these days, all began to pick up a little. Although there was no milk there was sugar and 1 ounce of sugar was worth a pound of the horse meat which had no fat and little food value.

On the night of the 24th/25th the steamer Julnar attempted to run past the Turks with supplies. Yearsley got secret orders at 7 p.m. to take a party of selected sappers with gangways and gear for tying up the ship to a selected landing place at the end of the Retrenched Line; where unloading and covering parties were also assembled. It was hoped that, after unloading, the ship would take back a mail and Yearsley was given many letters for dispatch.

After midnight, gun fire could be heard downstream and this got nearer and nearer: but at 1 a.m. it ceased; and it was guessed that the attempt had failed. The Julnar had in fact, after passing all the enemy positions, been stopped by two cables at Megassis, five miles downstream. She broke the first, but it stopped her way and the second fouled her rudder and she could not get away.

Yearsley got back at dawn.

Later the Julnar could be seen stranded downstream. Our five inch guns tried to destroy her but failed.

On the 25th and 26th everyone was very depressed, and realised that there was no hope left. There was no sign of action down stream. Early on the 26th, Gen. Townshend made arrangements to go to Megassis and see Khalil Pasha about the surrender but a Turk howitzer fired into Kut and he did not go. Apologies were sent in and on the 27th at day break, the General went down in a motor boat and arranged an armistice. He also had a private interview with Khalil and was believed to have offered the Turks a million pounds for the release of the garrison on parole from a humanitarian point of view; for the Turks were known to have little food.

All firing had, of course, ceased and it seemed very strange to be able to walk with safety above ground. There was a lot of discussion in messes as to the terms of surrender; everyone hoped for the best. Our men were very depressed at the prospect of surrender and Subedar Muhammad Din, meeting Brigadier General Evans, asked him why they could not go out and fight it out with the Turks.

On the 28th, General Townshend issued a communique saying that he hoped to arrange a surrender on parole; but in the afternoon, two staff officers who had gone to arrange terms came back with the news that the Turkish Government would only accept unconditional surrender. This was not announced till next day: but orders were issued in the afternoon to destroy all military stores except guns, rifles, and personal equipment. Of ammunition 30 rounds per gun and 250 per rifle were to be kept and the rest were thrown into the river this evening.

The gunners were particularly upset at the prospect of surrendering their guns and the officers of the 82nd Battery spent most of the night altering the cordite charges of their ammunition.

Early on the 29th orders came to destroy everything except 50 per cent of the rifles and corresponding ammunition which were to be kept as a defence against Arabs. There also came a last communique from Gen. Townshend to the effect that he was surrendering unconditionally but that he hoped still to arrange exchanges at Constantinople. He also thanked the troops for their devotion to duty.

In the morning, the 22nd Company helped the 82nd Battery to destroy their guns—using one slab of guncotton in the muzzle and one and a half in the breach, behind a shell, the breach block being closed as far as possible. This destruction was going on all over Kut. The result was like a general action. Bits of guns, rifles, shells, etc., were flying all over the place and it was wonderful no one was injured. As it was, the breach block of the A.A. Gun landed in the middle of the 17th Company's bivouac. The 22nd Company smashed their rifles with sledge hammers and the 17th used guncotton. A big fire was made and everything thrown on it that could be burnt, including saddlery. The officers destroyed all their kit except clothes. Actually they could have taken away a lot, as the Turks only searched the baggage once and that very indifferently.

At noon, the Union Jack was hauled down from the Serai and a white flag was hoisted. The Turks claimed to have the Union Jack, but it was actually destroyed or hidden. An order was issued to destroy the remaining rifles, but it never reached the companies.

At about 1 p.m. the Turks marched into Kut from the north-east with flags flying and shortly afterwards a detachment came into the Sappers' bivouac under a very pleasant young officer, took over our rifles and posted some sentries. The sappers had, of course, seen many Turks before, but none so ragged as these. No two were dressed alike; most of them were without boots or water bottles; many wore odd putties and their clothes were patched and patched again and "how they smelt!"

There was no looting in the Sapper lines. Turks were prowling about looking for boots and clothes but were apparently afraid of our men and would slink away if cursed at by an officer. The sentries were not bad fellows and behaved themselves during daylight and even at night they only did a little looting.

In Kut, however, things were very different. The sick and wounded in hospital were robbed of all they possessed and such of our men as could walk came back to the companies. Those who could not were particularly stripped naked. The Turkish officers did their best, shooting looters out of hand, but there were very few of them and the N.C.Os. were as bad as the men.

At 4 p.m., Matthews went into Kut with the men's pay documents, which were allowed to be sent back to India. Shortly afterwards orders were received that officers' swords were to be given up. This was a great blow as it had been hoped that they were going to be allowed to retain their swords. Orders were also received that the men could take away such kits as they could carry and the officers two hundred pounds. This sounded generous but actually kit was dropped all along the road to Turkey owing to lack of transport. At the time they reached Tekrit, the Sapper and Miner officers had only one change of clothes and one blanket apiece and three slept in one valise.

At about 6 p.m. the Turks tried to order the companies to move into the palm groves. As they could only communicate by signs, there was a good deal of misunderstanding, but luckily at this moment Matthews arrived back from Kut with comprehensible orders. The companies moved to the far end of the palm groves, to be ready to embark for Shumran next morning. The palm groves were already full of troops. The short move was very difficult. All kit and tents (to be used at Shumran) had to be carried. The men were desparately weak, darkness had set in and looting had become general. However it was completed by 10 p.m. The night passed pretty quietly in the Sappers' palm groves but all round looting was rife.

Tht emergency rations had been eaten on the 28th and 29th, and no more food had been issued.

At 5 a.m. on the 30th, the companies were ordered to the rivers' edge at 8 a.m. the 22nd Company with the Bridging Train and other troops were embarked in S.S. Basrah for Shumran, but the 17th Company sat in the sun all day while troops were slowly being moved. There was no food and all felt terribly ill with hunger and fatigue. Despite all that the officer could do, some men (both British and Indian) bartered their boots and water bottles for one or two Turkish ration buiscuits.

Meanwhile the Turks were hanging and mutilating Arabs, suspected of having helped the Pritish.

At 7 p.m., the 17th Company finally got up to Shumran. They had mostly lost all sense of what was happening and only just had strength to stagger on board.

So ended the siege of Kut-Al-Amara, of glorious and tragic memory and with it the exploits of the 6th Poona Division which now became for two and a half miserable years the "most sincere and precious guests of the Turkish Empire".

Naturally the siege was in most ways the least brilliant part of the work of the two field companies in Mesopotamia and the one period during which they did no actual fighting. It is doubtful if any Sapper fired his rifle during the siege. Nevertheless it was perhaps the supreme test of the men's discipline.

When Loring and Campbell were evacuated from Ctesiphon, there remained with the company no officer who had served with the Third Sappers and Miners before the war, though Matthews and Crawford had served with them since mobilization and had long considered themselves as Bombay Sappers. The following opinions are those of the D.E.C., his adjutant and Yearsley who commanded the 17th Company during the greater part of the siege, but had no previous connection with them.

Colonel Wilson says: as regards the morale of the Sappers, I am prepared to state difinitely that this was excellent throughout, whatever that of other troops may have been. Right up to the end, in spite of starvation rations they worked longer hours than any of the rest of the garrison.

Captain (Col.) Tomlinson writes: there is no doubt whatever that the morale of the Sappers was very high during the whole period of the siege. They had a great deal of work under most trying conditions and were always being turned out at night. In my opinion, no troops could have done better.

Lieut (Major) Yearsley summarizes his impressions as follows: in spite of living below ground level for months on end and being exposed to harassing fire whenever above ground: in spite of most of the work being at night and much of it in water, of a winter the cold and wet of which were a new experience to many and of rations gradually decreasing to starvation scale at a time when the nature of their work became increasingly heavy in connection with protection against flood and finally, in spite of disappointment after disappointment in their hopes of relief, there was never a moment when the uncomplaining endurance of the Sappers showed any sign of failure.

In the garrison generally, discipline was good. There was a little desertion among Mussalmans, a few cases of sleeping on sentry and a good deal of theft of food and wood. In the two field companies the only cases of serious crime recorded were the theft of three biscuits by a sentry, and one man severely punished for talking to Arabs about the state of the force.

Of individuals, Yearsley mentions in the 17th Company. Jemadar Fateh Khan as having done especially good work, Havildar Samundar Khan as the best N.C.O. in the company; Havildar Dewa Singh as absolutely fearless; Havildar Hari Chowdri as very good and Sapper Gajraj Singh (a Rajput and a great light weight wrestler) as the best sapper in the company.

In 22nd Company, Matthews says: that while all did well, Mathias and Subadar Mohammad Din were the outstanding figures.

The story of Kut prisoners of war is well known. Their sufferings were great especially during the march to Asia Minor, owing to the neglect and incapacity of the Turks rather than deliberate cruelty. Much of the dysentry which decimated the prisoners was due to the hard Turkish ration biscuit issued at Shumran. These were excellent for men in good condition but disastrous for men in the state of health of the garrison of Kut.

Short accounts by an Indian officer and an Indian N.C.O. of their captivity are given in the next chapter. Yearsley escaped to Cyprus (see "450 miles to Freedom") and one Indian, Sapper Wali Dad also escaped from Adana in 1917. The other survivors returned to India after the armistice. They were not formed again into the old companies whose numbers were given to two newly raised units, but as many as possible were drafted into the latter, which, it is hoped, will carry on their great tradition.

The surrender, of course, was the end of the war as far as 17th and 22nd Company were concerned; but three of their sister companies (18th, 20th and 21st) took their share in the revenge for Kut which followed in 1917 and in the final debacle of the Turks at Megiddo; and though the two Poona division companies could not participate in these events, they can claim to have borne their full share in earning the Royal title, which His Majesty the King Emperor conferred on their corps at the end of the Great War.

CHAPTER XV.

Below are printed two accounts of their captivity as prisoners of war, by Subadar Mohammad Din, Bahadur, I.O.M., (now Hon. Captain Mohammad Din, Sardar Bahadur, I.O.M.) and Naik (now Jemadar) Govind Bikhaji Dhure. It should be noted that the writer of the former was an officer and a Mohammadan and the latter a Hindu soldier. These accounts are printed without editing and without comment.

ACCOUNT OF CAPTIVITY IN TURKEY DURING THE GREAT WAR
BY
SUBADAR MOHAMMAD DIN, BAHADUR.

When we were taken prisoners by the Turks at Kut, we were brought to Shumran on ships, and were given ample food. The troops had starved for a long time during the siege, and when they suddenly got plenty of food many fell ill and died; the medical authorities said that this was due to their long abstinence and that they could not digest heavy food; and that they should be given light food only, such as rice etc. After about three days all the officer prisoners were roused suddenly at midnight, put on board a ship and taken to Baghdad. Here they were given a little money for private expenses. The rest of the troops were marched to Baghdad. The officers were sent by train from Baghdad to Shumran where they stayed for two days. Arab officers and guards of Arab soldiers went with us from Samarra to Aleppo. They treated the prisoners badly. Many lives were lost from cold and hunger because of their neglect, they did not value human life; if they saw anything of value on the prisoners, whether clothes or ornaments, they took it by force. On leaving Samarra some of the troops were fired on by Bedouins from the hills. In Baghdad many of the Arabs, men and women, whose relatives had been killed in the war, got very hostile and excited when they saw us.

From Shumran to Ras-Ul-Ain the generals were each given an arabia, or carriage and the other officers were supplied with donkeys to ride on. The remaining troops, with some doctors, marched on foot; they rested three days at Mosul but many men died on the way. From Mosul to Ras-Ul-Ain the officers were given mule carts, one cart to six officers. From Ras-Ul-Ain to Aleppo the prisoners were moved by rail; they stayed three days at Aleppo and the troops were given in the charge of a German railway company for work.

From Aleppo onwards the prisoners were in charge of regular Turkish guards and officers who treated the prisoners well. They were very kind hearted and valued and protected human life and property. We were given rations in accordance with the Corps Standing Orders of the Turkish Army. The officers were made to march over the Tarsus mountains from Tarsus to Bozanti with their baggage in carts; from there they went by train to Konia where the Hindu officers were imprisoned and the British and Mohammedan officers went on to Eski Shehir where the Mohammedan officers were detrained. Generals and full Colonels were sent to Broussa and the other British officers to Angora.

In the city of Eski Shehir we were given two storeyed houses which were clean and very good. These belonged to an Armenian contractor and we had to pay their rent. When complaints were made about this to the Turkish authorities they replied that there were no good Government houses to live in and therefore the houses had to be taken on lease, as there were a large number of prisoners to be accommodated.

At Eski Shehir we paid for bread, meat and vegetables out of the money allotted to each officer prisoner. Instead of firewood we were supplied with coal, which was free for warming but not for cooking purposes. Our sepoy orderlies received the same rations as the Turkish soldiers without any distinction. In this city the arrangements were good as it was a very big Turkish Station and there were many senior Turkish officers there. Both here and at Broussa the troops got their clothing from the Turks and the officers received clothing from England in addition to Rs. 12 per month. We got cash from the Turks as well for our food which was quite sufficient to meet our requirements. A sepoy prisoner was allowed for every two officers to cook their food; this orderly went daily to the bazaar to buy the necessaries of life under the supervision of the Turkish guards. The officers had also to pay their rent out of these allowances. They were allowed to go for a stroll twice daily with Turkish guards from nine to eleven and from five to six.

After a year we were sent to Broussa where the generals had already been stationed; here we were made to live in an American School along with Generals Evans, Delamain, Hamilton and Melliss. General Townshend also was on an island nearby. Here we were not required to pay rent.

After peace was made the Ottoman Government published an order that officers and soldiers who wished to stay in Turkey would be allowed to do so. They would be given two plots of land each and two bullocks, a house to live in, a garden and a shop. They would also be allowed to marry. We were then taken by sea to Taranto in Italy. Here the British Officers were disembarked and we were sent to Egypt where we were handed over to the British authorities.

NOTE. It should be borne in mind that the Mohammedan officers were interned separately from the other Indian officers and received better treatment.

Account of Captivity in Turkey During the Great War
by
Naik Govind Bikhaji Dhure.

On the 30th April 1916, we marched from Kut to Shumran camp in two lots, one going by boat and the other on foot. This camp, Shumran, where we had been sent to, was about 7 miles from Kut, and there we were given rations by the Turks, which had been despatched for our troops and had been captured by the Turks. We were kept in this camp for three days and the British and Indian officers were separated from us. One donkey was given to every two officers for transport. On the 4th day, we other ranks and also the followers, each with his own bedding on his back, started the march to Baghdad.

The Turks knew that we had suffered very severe hunger and therefore could not do a very long march, so they made a camp in jungle wherever water was available. The Turkish arrangements for this march were that a few troops, who were Baddoos or Khurds, remained round us, and with them were a few ponies on which rations were loaded for use at places where none could be obtained.

These were the only arrangements made for our custody. The commander of our guard was a 2nd Lieutenant, who had with him an Arab Major.

On the first day, the 4th May 1916, we marched off at 12 o'clock, and having marched a few miles, pitched camp before the evening. We had rations with us for that evening.

On the 5th May 1916, we arrived at Baghdadieh where we were given bread and dates, but insufficient of both. We mixed the bread and dates, and ate them. We tried to give English money to get these things. Our rupees were not accepted. After that we started giving spare clothing.

On the 6th May 1916, we again marched and camped for the night in the jungle.

On the 7th we arrived at Aziziyeh and stayed there for a two days' rest; we were given unripe wheat and meat, but we did not know how to eat them. Eventually we discovered that the wheat and meat should be mixed together and cooked. We had no cooking utensils, but each man had a ration tin; we collected grass and leaves from near by and each man prepared his own food.

In Turkish this is called bulgur yemak, and by us pillau.

On the morning of the 10th May we marched on. This was the worst day for us and the heat was very great. No halts were made and the water in our water bottles had already been finished. When any one managed to get water from a river, he drank his fill. In another place we saw a great many Arabs coming running towards us. They were all carrying drawn swords. We were wondering who these people were. Then they came near and started to stare at us. They then shouted in Arabic and danced. They also spat upon us. After this long march we camped in the jungle near Lajj. This day we got Turkish Army biscuits, made of dried barley bread, about four inches in diameter and three quarters of an inch thick. Each man got two, but they were as hard as wood and those with weak teeth could not bite them, so we soaked them in warm water and they became soft like chappattis.

They should be eaten with tea, of which I had forgotten the very name at the time we were captured.

On the morning of the 11th May we marched into Baghdad. I rejoiced at seeing Baghdad, but regretted seeing it as a prisoner.

We entered Baghdad at about one o'clock, and went straight through the bazaars to the Railway Station, where we pitched camp. There was difficulty in getting water here. There was one tap in the station where there was a large crowd.

Finally, the order for drawing water was withdrawn, and it was difficult to exist without water.

Anyone trying to draw water was beaten by the sentry. By the grace of God we managed to live through the day.

On the morning of the 12th May we started off by rail, to Samarra, where we arrived at 2 o'clock and pitched camp on the River Tigris. We stayed here until the 15th May and met our British and Indian Officers, who were encamped about a mile away from us. They had been given Turkish money, but the other ranks had even had to sell their spare clothes.

On the 15th May we again marched off, and arrived in Takrit on the afternoon of the 16th. Here the inhabitants came two miles to look at us prisoners.

We were very pleased to see that they had brought water with them, but we discovered that they meant to sell it, not to give it to us.

When Mussalmans asked them for water they replied "Jib flus". They would not take English money for it, neither would they give it away free to anyone.

Whoever tried to take water was beaten with whips. We pitched camp in Takrit on the banks of the River Tigris, and people came to sell us bread. How could we poor hungry prisoners buy it? and is it any wonder that some started to take it from them by force?

In this town, Takrit, we had field dressings, like sky blue handkerchiefs, fixed with a safety pin and these proved very useful. In exchange for a handkerchief we got eight pieces of bread and for a pin, four or five. Mussalmans bought flour to make bread, and Hindus flour and dates, while the English bought whatever they could get.

On the evening of 17th May, we marched in the direction of Mosul, leaving some of our sick and one or two doctors behind in Takrit.

On the morning of the 18th we pitched camp in the jungle about 25 miles away. This appeared to be a fairly fertile district, there being fields of corn and barley. We broke off the stalks and eat our full of them. We got Turkish biscuits in this camp.

We camped in the jungle again on the 19th and arrived in Sher Gat on the 20th. Near this camp was a fort where the Turkish Sepoys had a mosque. Here we were given fresh bread, made of barley and with it uncooked gram, but we did not know how to eat it with bread.

Except for our ration tins, we had no eating utensils so we parched the gram and put it in our haversacks, and kept it in readiness for our march to the next camp. This was a very short march, perhaps only about 10 miles. We started off and arrived after about a four hours march.

In this camp we were given goat's flesh and bread, but we had no salt, chillies etc., and could obtain none in this place.

There were no spare Turkish supplies. What salt there was left among us was collected and put on the meat and we then cooked and ate it.

We marched on on the 21st May at 4 o'clock. We were told that the march would only be a four hour one, and were pleased that we should get some sleep this night. Unfortunately the water at the camp was brackish. This day was the worst of all.

Only those people who have made a forced march as a prisoner can realise what it was like.

Since the water was bad and we were told that it would only be a four hours march, no one took water. Having started at 4 o'clock we kept marching all night, and there was no sign of a camp. Finally, we, hungry, helpless, sick and tired prisoners started asking for water. But there was no water, water from the pakhals strapped to the horses could not be got without money. People now began to fall and die of thirst. I cannot give an accurate account, but I am sure that 80 people must have died, through lack of food and water. When morning came with no sign of camp, and men began to fall by the way side, a Turkish officer ordered that whoever could go on was to go, but not to leave the road. We would reach water in two hours.

A full glass of water cost from eight annas to one rupee and eight annas.

Havildar Saknak Honnak had a golden ring of 1½ tolas. He sold it to a sowar who gave him four annas for it, but returned it later as brass and took back his four annas. Havildar Saknak Honnak thanked God and distributed eight annas worth of dates to his friends.

The first two to reach the water were Havildar Abdul Khan of the 104th Rifles, and L/Naik Ali Haider Shah, 22nd Field Company. These two came back and told us to cheer up and go ahead, as there was water in the nullah near the hill. We took our water bottles and filled them. The very thirsty were given water drop by drop.

This water saved the lives of several men. After taking a little rest we marched on again, and at two o'clock arrived in camp, having buried our dead comrades as well as we could. This march had been forty miles.

Here we met the Turkish Army which was coming to support the Army in Kut. We remained here for the day and night of the 22nd and marched on again on the morning of the 23rd arriving in Hamam Ali, where there was a hot water spring.

We remained here for the rest of that day and for the night and reached Mosul next day after a very short march. In Mosul we were divided into three, Mussalmans, Hindus, and English, and separated. The English marched off first followed by the Mussalmans and then Hindus. The first camp after Mosul was about fifteen miles away on the banks of the Tigris River.

After this we left the river, and the second march was to Tel Hadi, where the English troops were halted. The next day the Mussalmans reached this place and were also halted, similarly the Hindus on the third day. The reason for halting thus was that the Turkish Commander—Anwar Pasha was to inspect the prisoners. We were fallen in in three parties and he inspected us at 8 o'clock in the morning; he talked with some Indian Troops in Persian and asked them if they had enrolled before or during the war

He then inspected the English Troops, and after that he stood with his staff between the three parties, and asked in a loud voice whether any of the English knew French. A man from the Dorsets Regiment fell out and went up to him, and was asked whether he had had any trouble, if so to say what it was. He said that they were having serious trouble from the Major who was commanding them. He said that the latter did not give out rations and water fairly, and that when any of the troops became tired and faint on the march and asked for water, this major's sepoy would not give it to them without money; also that when any one became faint through thirst and sat down, he was beaten till he collapsed senseless, and was left for dead.

When Anwar Pasha heard this, he spoke angrily to the major concerned. We were unable to understand what the English soldier had been saying.

After that day there was an improvement, and when any one asked for water on the march, they were given it, and the tired and sick were allowed to go at their own slow pace.

The third march was about 25 miles, to a place called Tel Aman, the fourth camp was Halwa, the fifth Nisbin, the sixth Sar Jaman, the seventh Jorab and the eighth was Ras-Ul-Ain.

After a week or two, while in Ras-Ul-Ain, working parties were told off for special railway work. The Turk is incapable of making a bandobast and so the railway had only got to Ras-Ul-Ain.

When the Germans saw the prisoners, they started work on the railway. The Hindus of the 17th and 22nd Field Companies were formed into two parties, with Havildar Pandu Deokar and Naik Balwant Singh in one, and Havildar Ramdin Tiwari in the other, and having about 150 men under them.

When we were given this work we were all very weak. The frost and cold were felt very much as we had few clothes and little strength. As I mentioned before we had sold our clothes for food on the way. Ten or twelve of our troops died here. Doctor Captain Puri Sahib and Vittal Satputte did much valuable work in saving lives in this place, and we Indians should have been in a bad way without them, as there was no proper Turkish hospital in Ras-Ul-Ain. Havildar Tatiya Sawant acted as an adjutant in this camp, and gave every sort of help to his Hindu companions. (Tatiya Sawant Sahib is now subedar of the 4/5th Mahrattas). In Ras-Ul-Ain we were given at least one and half lbs. of atta and two to four ounces of gram or wheat. The hours of work were from six in the morning till six in the evening. There were no arrangements for cooking, and no check was kept on the prisoners as there were no special sentries. We had Arab blankets for sleeping. After three or four months I and many others became ill and were sent further on to Gelawag. It appeared to be not more than ten or twelve miles in the tram and there was a shortage of coal. When I got out at Gelawag I saw that there was at least 25—30 miles of tramway. The speed of this tram was about 6—8 miles an hour, the reason for it being so slow being that it had to go on a very round about circuit.

When I got out at Balamadi, the Turks behaved with great cruelty and cut the hairs of our Sikhs. There were many rumours concerning this affair, but what could prisoners do? If they resisted they were killed, and fearing death they did nothing.

After 3-4 days in the train on from Balamadi we got out at Alu Kaisha East station where we were told there was a three day's march ahead of us. This march was along a track through hilly country; those who became weak and sick were killed, since they could not walk, and buried in a nullah with a stone on them; Sapper Govind Sindhe of 22nd Company was among these.

Our destination was Bhor, where we kept for 4-5 months. Here rations became scarce and the sick were marched on to Afrion Kara Hissar, where we were strictly confined like real prisoners, being kept in a fort under proper supervision. Here we had little comfort and hardship became greater. In this fort a captain was in charge, whom we named Billa. This captain beat a man in the 66th Punjab Regiment to death, and was punished for this by being reduced to the ranks by sentence of a court-martial. After 2 or 3 months of medical treatment, those of us who were fit went back by train to Kala Bagh, to work. We did 6-8 months of work on the Tramway Railway in Kala Bagh. The feeding arrangements in this place were that those who went on work got rations; those who reported sick were either given sick leave, or sent back on work; neither of these got rations.

With our bread we got wheat, and sometimes Bakla seeds. There was a German Major commanding in this place who had spent 10—12 years in India. Hearing him talk Urdu, we tried to find out how he knew it and where he learnt it. He told us that he had served for 10—12 years in a Russian Company in India, and had seen all India. We then asked him why he fed us in the way he did, when he must surely have seen the Army's feeding arrangements in India. He replied that he could only give those things to eat which were authorized by the Turkish authorities. There was a Railway Station in this place where we met our prisoner friends who were coming up from the rear. Here also we met a Turkish force coming down from the North, who, on seeing us, became very angry and came up to strike us.

Thus we spent our days in Kalabagh until 11th November 1918, when news of peace came through. The sentries were removed from us.

After that we used to play ordinary games there. On the 16th November an English Major arrived in an empty train from the direction of Halab (Aleppo); seeing our blankets by the edge of the line he stopped the train and came up to us. We got in the train there and after three days reached Tarsus where we spent the day and night on the banks of the river and embarked on a ship at 8 next morning. After three days we reached Alexandria and coming from there we met many of our Indian comrades and received gifts. We then went by train to the Suez Canal where the 18th Field Company were.

Many people at that time were weak and sick. After three or four days we got the order to embark; there were seven sappers there at that time, who were the first party of prisoners. We arrived in Bombay at 8 a.m. on the 5th January 1919, and, being the first ship carrying home prisoners, large crowds had collected to meet us.

At that time all we wished for was to go to our homes and meet our friends.

On the 7th January at 7 o'clock, two Sikhs of 17th Company, three Mussalmans of 22nd Company and Naik Govind Bhikaji Dhure stepped out of the mail train at Kirkee station.

On the 8th at 11 o'clock we paraded in front of the Park Guard to meet Colonel Colvin.

Those who were prisoners will never forget it, even after death. The other ranks of the 17th and 22nd Companies were very sorry that their British officers were separated from them. This was a great misfortune.

Now at this time, there are five of us who were prisoners, still serving. They are Jemadar Samundar Khan, Jemadar Govind Dhure, Havildar Ali Haidar Shah, Havildar Laxuman Vachakal and Sapper Roshan Khan.

I expect that in a few years there will be no one left in the Corps who was in the war in 1914—15, nor any of the old British officers either. This will be a great pity

My history is now finished.

Appendix III.

Organiation of Field Companies, Sappers and Miners in 1914.

The war establishment of a field company in 1914 was:—

British officers, (R.E.) ...	4
Indian officers. ...	3 (One Subedar and two Jemadars).
British N.C.Os. (R.E.)	2

Indian other ranks:—

Havaldars	6
Naiks	10
Sappers	150
Buglers	2
Ward orderly	1
Driver havaldar ...	1
,, naik.	1
Sapper drivers ...	18
	189
Mules	18

These were organized in four sections, each about 45 strong and each with four equipment mules carrying tools and explosives and led by sapper drivers. The rest of the company's engineer equipment was normally carried in Army Transport carts.

The class composition of all companies of the Third Sappers and Miners was officially:—

2 sections Punjabi Mussalmans.
1 ,, Mahrattas.
1 ,, Sikhs.

But this had only lately been adopted. The Sikh section of the 17th Company was mostly composed of Rajputs while both companies had one section of mixed Hindus and Mussalmans, chiefly from the United Provinces. The actual composition on mobilization therefore was:—

17th Company.

Right half—	No. 1 section		Punjabi Mussalmans.
,,	,, 2	,,	Mixed.
Left half—	,, 3	,,	Mahrattas.
,,	,, 4	,,	Rajputs with a few Sikhs.

22nd Company.

Right half—	No. 1 section		Sikhs.
,,	,, 2	,,	Mixed.
Left half—	,, 3	,,	Mahrattas.
,,	,, 4	,,	Punjabi Mussalmans.

Appendix IV.

Statistics.

British officers.

Embarked with companies.	...	8
Joined in Mesopotamia.	...	7
		15
Killed in action or died of wounds.		5
Wounded and invalided to India.		4
Prisoners of war (3 had been wounded).		6
		15

Indian officers.

Embarked with companies.	...	6
Joined in Mesopotamia.	...	1
Promoted in Mesopotamia.	...	5
		12
Killed in action or died of wounds.		3
Wounded and invalided.	...	3
Invalided sick.	...	2
Prisoners of war. (2 wounded.)		4
		12

British N.C.Os.

Embarked with companies	...	4	4
Invalided sick.	...	1	
Prisoners of war (all had been wounded).		3	4

All the above prisoners of war survived to be released at the armistice.

Indian other Ranks.

The statistics of Indian other Ranks are very incomplete. The following is an attempted reconstruction. It is believed to be nearly correct. It is certain that no figure is overstated.

17th Company.

Proceeded with company to Mesopotamia.	209
Joined from drafts.	124
	333
Promoted to commissioned rank. ...	3
Killed or died of wounds.	8
Died of disease before surrender. ...	9
Invalided to India.	155
Died while prisoners of war.	41
Released prisoners of war.	116
Prisoners of war.—escaped.	1
	333

22nd Company.

Proceeded with company to Mesopotamia.	208
Joined from drafts.	123
	331
Promoted to commissioned rank. ...	2
Killed or died of wounds.	27
Died of disease before surrender. ...	21
Invalided to India.	109
Died while prisoners of war.	59
Released prisoners of war.	113
	331

The numbers wounded and the number among the invalided who were evacuated on account of wounds is unknown. One man of 17th Company and two of 22nd Company were evacuated from Kut after its surrender.

The statistics re followers are even more scanty. When the siege began there were 34 followers with the two companies; of these one was killed during the siege, one died as prisoner of war and 32 were released.

Appendix V.

Honours and Distinctions Awarded.

			Company.
Distinguished Service Order.	Captain	A. B. Matthews. R.E.	22
	Lieut.	W. H. Mathias, 128th Pioneers attached.	22
Military Cross.	Lieut.	M. G. G. Campbell, R.E.	17
	,,	A. B. Matthews, R.E.	22
	Captain	E. J. Loring, R.E.	17
	,,	R. C. Lord, R.E,	17
	,,	K. D. Yearsley, R.E.	17
Order of British India 2nd Class.	Subadar	Baryam Singh, I.O.M.	17
	,,	Muhamad Din, I.O.M.	22
Indian Order of Merit 1st Class.	Jemadar	Ramswami Naidu.	22
	2878 Naik	Son Singh.	22
Indian Order of Merit 2nd Class.	Jemadar	Feroz Ali.	22
	2855 Naik	Dalip Singh.	22
	2672 Havildar	Ghulam Nabi.	17
	3747 L/Naik	Nur Dad.	17
	3898 Sapper	Ghulam Haidar.	17
	Jemadar	Ramswami Naidu.	22
	,,	Muhamad Din.	17
	4193 Sapper	Hari Tingre.	17
	2878 ,,	Son Singh.	22
	3955 Naik	Sayad Hussain.	22
	3625 ,,	Hardat Singh.	22

	4067	Sapper	Indar Singh.	22
	4587	,,	Abdul Aziz.	22
	3075	,,	Indar Singh.	22
Indian Distin-	2268	Havildar	Fateh Khan.	17
guished Service	1930	,,	Gangajirao	
Medal.			Khanvilkar.	22
	2897	Naik	Narayan Halatkar.	22
	3955	L/Naik	Sayad Hussain.	22
	2151	Havildar	Khrishna Bhonsle.	17
	4012	L/Naik	Bagga Singh.	17
	3876	Havildar	Samundar Khan.	17
	3111	Sapper	Gajraj Singh.	17
	3953	Havildar	Mohd Din Khan.	22
	3773	C.H.M.	Mahmud Khan	22
	3876	Naik	Sawla Thopte.	22
Bar to I.D.S.M.	3376	Havildar	Samundar Khan.	17
Meritorious	1971	Havildar	Dewa Singh.	17
Service Medal.	3175	Naik	Sukha Singh.	17
	3178	L/Naik	Allah Baksh.	17
	2560	Sapper	Rama Pidraya.	22
	3004	,,	Shaikh Burhan.	22
	2586	C.H.M.	Ramadin Tiwari,	22

The following honours awarded may also be combined as pertaining to the two 3rd Sappers and Miners Companies.

Lt-Col. U. W. Evans, R.E.   Companionship of St. Michael and St. George.

Companionship of the Bath.

Mentions in Despatches.

41 names from 17th Company and 34 from 22nd Company were mentioned in despatches. In addition the 17th Company itself was mentioned three times and the 22nd Company twice in the bodies of despatches.

INDEX.

A.

Abadan	2
Abdul Aziz, Spr.	77, 131
Abdul Khan, Hav.	121
Afrion Kara Hissar	123
Ahwaz	22
Akaika Channel	38
Aleppc	115, 116, 124
Ali Gharbi	37, 85
Ali Haidar Shah, L/N.	121, 124
Allah Bakhsh, Spr.	131
Alloa	20
Alu Kaisha	123
Amara	29, 32, Chapter VI
Angora	116
Anwar Pasha (Enver)	121, 122
Arbuthnot, Capt. A.D.S.	2, 3, 5, 6, 98
Aronda, (Hired transport)	2
Arter, Sgt.	1
Asani	38
Ashar	8
Ataba Marsh	43
Aylmer, General	85
Aziziyah	46, 50, 65, 67, 118

B.

Bagga Singh, L/N.	131
Baghdad	115, 117, 119,
Baghdadieh	118
Bahrein	1
Bait Aessa	107, 108, 109
Baker. Sgt.	2, 40, 72
Balamadi	123
Balwant Singh, Nk.	122
Barjasiyeh Wood	25
Barker, Major	84, 90
Barrett, Lt. General Sir A.	3
Baryam Singh, Subr.	2, 66, 72, 83, 108, 130
Basra	2, 7, 8, 9, et seq.

ii.

Batteries, 82nd R.F.A., 17, 68, 74, 83, 110, 111, S. R.H.A. 75
   ,,   65th   ,, ... 24
   ,,   76th   ,, ... 24, 57
   ,,   23rd Mountain 26
   ,,   Hants, ... 68
Bellis, Sgt. 1, 43, 72, 75
Bhor 123
"Billa" 123
Bombay Volunteer Artillery 84
Boyes, Lt. W.R. ... ... 41 to 93
Bozanti 116
Bridging Train, Bengal S. & M.   20, 42, 50, 51, 52, 57, 64
                                         65, 67, 71, 75, 76, 86, 112
Broussa 116, 117
Bustan 55
Butterfly, H.M.S. 66

C.

Campbell, Lt. M.G.G. ... ... 2 to 130
Cavalry, 25th Light 25
Cavalry, 16th 67
Cheshire Lt. H.S.   63, 72, 77, 83, 85, 93, 96, 103
Chowharja Baksh Singh, Jem. ... 37, 39
Clery's Post 44
Colbeck, Capt. C.E. 20, 71, 81
Cookson, Cmdr. R.N. 46
Crawford, Lt. K.B.S. ... ... 2 to 113
Ctesiphon ... ... 53, Chapter X

D.

Dalip Singh, Naik (Hav.) 4, 83, 130
Darhamiyeh 27
Delamain, Brigadier Gen. W.S. ... 1 to 117
Dewa Singh, Hav. 114, 131
Diyalah River 53
Dorsets, 2nd Bn. ...   1, 4, 22, 24, 44, 45, 58, 74
Dujailah Redoubt 43, 97, 98
Dunhill, Lt. C.M.G. ... ... 1 to 68

E.

East, Lt. A.T. ... ... 41 to 83
Eski Shehir 116
Es-Sinn ... ... 42 to 143
Evans, Lt. Col. U.W. (Brigadier Gen.) ... 2 to 131
Ezra's Tomb 32

F.

Fao	2
Fateh Khan, Hav. (Jem.)	18, 19, 28, 72, 83, 86, 114, 131
Firoz Ali, Jem. (Sub.)	1, 4, 7, 26, 27, 28, 130
"Flatulent Flossie"	63, 94
Flood Control, Basra	11
Flood Protection, Kut	91 et seq
Frazer, Lt. Col.	17
Fry, Maj. Gen.	18, 45

G

Gajraj Singh, Spr.	114, 131
Gangajirao Khanvilkar, Hav. (Jem.)	41, 131
Ganpatrao Jahdao, Jem.	2, 37
Garrett, Lt.	28, 36, 50, 60, 102
Gelawag	122, 123
Ghulam Nabi, Hav.	17, 18, 130
Ghulam Haider, Spr.	17, 18, 130
Gorringe, Maj. Gen.	38, 40, 103, 105
Govind Bhikaji Dhure, Nk. (Jem.)	115, 117, 129
Govind Sindhe, Spr.	123
Gribbon, Capt.	76, 77
Gurkha Mound	61, 62
Gurkha, Rifles 2/7th	40, 61, 77, 96

H.

Hala	20
Halwa	122
Hamam Ali	121
Hamilton, Brigadier Gen.	55, 58, 59, 74, 117
Hammar Lake	38
Hampshire Regiment, 3rd Bn.	39
Hardat Singh, Nk.	130
Hari Tingre, Spr.	39, 41, 130
Hewett, Capt.	39
Hoghton, Brigadier Gen.	44, 49, 55, 59, 62, 73
Horse Shoe Marsh	43
Huzzars, 14th	65

I.

Ilam Din, Hav.	18
Indar Singh, Spr. (L/N.)	77, 131
Indar Singh, Spr.	101, 131
Infantry, 119th	25, 57, 81
,, 120th	24, 58

J.

Jala	20
Jahala Canal	34, 35
Jawahir Singh, Hav.	47
Jorab	122
Julnar, S.S.	42, 46, 109, 110

K.

Kala Bagh	123, 124
Keru Jamdade, Sub.	1, 4, 7
Khalil Bey. General	63, 110
Khrishna Bhonsle, Hav. (Jem.)	47, 72, 83, 131
Kiln Post, Shaiba	24
Konia	116
Kumait	36
Kut-Al-Amara	42, 46, 71, et seq
Kutuniyeh	51, 52, 67

L.

Lajj	52, 63, 64, 118
Lancers, 7th	25
Lord, Lt. R.C.	2, 18, 19, 25, 38, 39, 40. 41, 130
Loring, Capt. E.J.	19 to 130
Laxuman Vachakal, Hav.	124

M.

Madras S. & M. 12th Field Coy.	38
Mahrattas, 117th	1, 2, 4, 24, 26, 44, 45, 100
Mahratta Light Infantry, 110th	17, 18, 19, 24, 26, 58
,, ,, ,, 103rd	81, 84, 96
Mahmud Khan, C.H.M.	131
Majanina Creek	39
Mason, Capt. K.	98
Mathias, Lt. W.H.	72 to 130
Matthews, Lt. A.B.	1 to 130
Mazera	17, 18, 20
Megassis	86
Melliss, Major Gen.	24, 26, 55, 67, 74, 77, 96, 97, 117
Molesworth, Capt. F.C.	3, 9
Moreland, Capt.	56
Mosul	116, 119, 121
Muhammad Din, Jem. (Sub.)	2, 27, 39, 47, 72, 106, 110, 114, 115, 130
Musharra Canal	34
Muzaibila	19

N.

Nahairat	30
Nahrwan Canal	56
Nakaila	22
Nakhailat	43
Narayan Halatkar, Nk.	131
Nasiriyeh	22, Chapter VII
Nisbin	122
Nixon, Gen. Sir J.	31, 43, 65, 66
Norfolks, 2nd Bn.	5, 17, 24, 58, 59, 84
Nunn, Capt. R.N.	31
Nur Dad, L/N.	17, 18, 130
Nur Khan, Spr.	24

O.

Oxford Light Infantry	32, 59, 84

P.

Pandu Deokar, Hav.	122
Pioneers 48th	3, 23, 24, 39, 57, 71, 80, 84, 92. 98, 101, 107
Punjabis 20th	1, 4
,, 22nd	57, 59, 101
,, 24th	24, 26, 61
,, 67th	76, 77
,, 76th	55, 57, 62
Puri, Capt.	122

Q.

Qalat Saleh	32
Qala Shadi	68
Qurna	10, Chapter III, 29, et seq,

R.

Rajputs, 7th	5, 58
Rama Piraya, Spr.	131
Ramdin Tiwari, Hav.	122, 131
Ramswami Naidu, Jem. (Sub.)	1, 27, 28, 45, 47, 130
Ras-Ul-Ain	116, 122
Rifles, 104th	1, 4, 17, 19, 24, 58, 100
Rimington, Maj. Gen.	71
Robat Crek	10
Roshan Khan, Spr.	124
Royal West Kents, 2nd Bn.	39, 65
Ruta Canal	20

S.

Sadar Din, Jem.	21
Sahain	3
Sahil, action at	3 et seq
Saknak Honak, Hav.	121
Samarra	115, 119
Samundar Khan, Hav.	114, 129, 131
Sandes, Capt. E.W.C.	26, 65, 76, 77
Sanaiya	2
Sar Jaman	122
Sawla Thopie, Nk.	131
Sayad Hussain, Naik	130, 131
Searchlight Section	23
Shaiba	21, Chapter IV
Shaikh Burhan, Spr.	131
Shaikh Saad	42, 85
Shankaram Pille, Hav. (Jem.)	47, 59, 72
Shat-Al-Arab	2
Shumran	112, 113, 114, 116, 117
Shergat	120
Shwaiyib Creek	17
Sirmur Sappers and Miners	20, 21, 31, 34, 71, 73, 81, 100
Sohan Singh, Spr. (Nk.)	45, 77, 130
South Salient, Shaiba	22, 23
Spink, Lt.	68, 72, 84, 91, 100
Stace, Capt.	73, 76, 84, 101
Sukha Singh, Nk.	131
Suleman Askari, Turkish Gen.	22, 27
Sumana, River Steamer	39, 74, 76, 101
Sunnaiyat	42, 105, 106, 109
Suwada Marsh	43
Suwaikiya Marsh	44
Sweet, Lt.	77, 78

T.

Takrait	119
Taranto	117
Tarsus	116, 124
Tatya Sawant Hav.	122
Tek Singh, Hav. (Jem.)	7, 47
Tel Aman	122
Tel Hadi	121
Toleman, Sgt.	2, 40, 72, 101
Tomlinson, Capt. H.W.	23, 24, 84, 95, 113

Townshend's Regatta	...	...	... 29
Townshend, Maj. Gen.	...	...	31 to 117
Twiss, Capt. A M.	...	...	1, 4, 6

U.

Umaria, (hired transport)	...	...	... 2
Um-At-Tabul	...	...	... 67
Utterson. Maj.	...	...	... 60

V.

Varela (hired transport)	...	...	1, 66
Vital Point	...	...	53, 55, 58. 59
Vittal Satpute	...	...	... 122

W.

Wali Dad, Spr.	...	...	... 114
Water Redoubt	...	...	55, 59, 62, 65
Whiteley, Lt. E.C.	...	1, 3,	24, 25, 27, 28
Whiteley's Bridge	...	...	... 12
Wilson, Col. F.A.	...	...	60 to 113
Wingfield Smith, Capt.	...	...	... 102
Winsloe, Maj. A.R.	...		3, 5, 20, 33, 90
Woolpress Village	...	...	73, 97, 101

Y.

Yearsley, Lt. K.D.	...	...	85 to 130

Z.

Zubair	...	...	...	... 22